MISSION to OZ

Reaching
Postmoderns
Without Losing
Your Way

MISSION
OZ
to

Mark Tabb

MOODY PUBLISHERS
CHICAGO

L. Frank Baum's novel *The Wonderful Wizard of Oz* (George M. Hill Company, 1900) is the source of references about Oz.

All Scripture quotations, unless otherwise indicated, are taken from the *Holy Bible, New Living Translation,* copyright © 1996. Used by permission of Tyndale House Publishers, Inc., Wheaton, Illinois 60189. All rights reserved.

Scripture quotations marked NIV are taken from the *Holy Bible, New International Version®.* NIV®. © 1973, 1978, 1984 by International Bible Society. Used by permission of Zondervan Publishing House. All rights reserved.

Library of Congress Cataloging-in-Publication Data

Tabb, Mark A.
    Mission to Oz : reaching postmoderns without losing your way / Mark Tabb.
    p. cm.
    Includes bibliographical references (p.   ).
    ISBN 0-8024-4293-5
    1. Evangelistic work. 2. Postmodernism—Religious aspects—Christianity. I. Title.

BV3793.T33 2004
269'.2—dc22

                    2004000166

1 3 5 7 9 10 8 6 4 2

Printed in the United States

> "BUCKLE YOUR SEAT BELT, DOROTHY,
> 'CAUSE KANSAS IS GOING BYE-BYE."
> CYPHER IN *THE MATRIX*

Contents

Foreword   9
Acknowledgments   13

PART 1
WELCOME TO OZ
1. I Have a Feeling We're Not in Kansas Anymore   17
2. Riding the Cyclone   23
3. One of Everything, Please   31
4. Strawberry Fields Lie Just to the Left of   39
   the Yellow Brick Road
5. Hands-on and High-Touch   49
6. "I Saw the Potato"   59

PART 2
A BRAIN, A HEART, DA' NERVE
7. Pay No Attention to That Man Behind the Curtain 69
8. X Faith   77

9. The Real World   85
10. A Reason for Being   95

PART 3
WIZARD OR HUMBUG?

11. Do Something   105
12. More than Words   109
13. Face-to-Face   117
14. Coming Out from Behind the Curtain   127

Postscript: In the Arena   137
Appendix A: Recommended Books   143
Appendix B: Learning to Hear the Message   147
Notes   151

Foreword

"I'm not asking you take them out of the world, but to keep them safe from the evil one. They are not part of this world any more than I am. Make them pure and holy by teaching them your words of truth. As you sent me into the world, I am sending them into the world"
—a prayer of Jesus, John 17:15–18.

Here's a dose of honesty.

When I'm close to God, I feel at odds with this world in which I live. Yet, during those times when I have drifted away from Him, well, that's when I think that this world is just peachy and believe that it can make me happy.

That being the case for all Christians, we should strive to be aware that this world is NOT our home, and its ways and pursuits shouldn't be ours either.

C. S. Lewis commented that this "out of place" feeling that Christians experience is because we are all really longing for our "true country." His term, "true country" has always struck me. When I think of my country, I'm so thankful to be an American. Despite how it has fallen, I still believe it's a blessed land with a rich heritage of faith. The problem with living in such a great country is that it can be such a pleasing land that even we Christians (who are supposed to be longing for our "true country") start to feel completely at home here.

Eventually, though, every Christian should take to heart that this world is not our home and that we will be finally and eternally blessed at our next stop. Heaven!

So . . . what do we do in the meantime? Here we are on earth, surrounded by people who are *very* "at home" here. Their goals are all about this life. Their pursuits are mostly about the temporary pleasures they can receive. Even their most outrageous and wildest dreams stay pretty much confined to what can take place here on earth.

Pretty soon they too realize they're not satisfied. This world just doesn't cut it. They want more. They go from one activity to another trying to fill this void. Maybe a new diet. Maybe a new hobby. A new relationship, perhaps. Despite their efforts, nothing really satisfies their hunger. The problem is, *they don't know what they need.* They're depressed and sad. Many are desperate. In short, they're lost.

In *Mission to Oz* Mark Tabb defines the task that Christians are called to perform as we co-exist on earth with people who are lost. Frankly, we have the answer they need, but we have a hard time trying to figure out how to reach them—let alone muster up the courage to do so. We think things like, "they're so different from us" or "we can't relate to them," or "they would never understand where we're coming from."

We have put up a huge wall between "them" and "us." In our minds there's an impassable barrier between the "saved" and the "lost."

Mark Tabb's understanding of the postmodern world and his advice on how postmodern Christians are to reach out to the lost are valuable tools for all believers. He hammers home the truth that God isn't surprised with our current situation. God remains well aware that we are in many ways "fish out of water" on this planet. Mark's challenge is for us to do as the Wizard of Oz did and "come out from behind the curtain." I really appreciate his stance that we believers need to stop being intimidated and just get real with people. They've heard a lot about religion and have grown cold and skeptical. They desire something real that will change their life. Their inability to find it on their own has caused them great frustration and pain. The remedy for their pain comes in the form of authentic and Christlike love. It is powerful and has proved to soften the hardest and most wicked of hearts throughout history (mine included)!

I appreciate Mark Tabb because he has encouraged me (and you will be encouraged as well) with *Mission to Oz*. There has never been a better time in history to reach the world for Christ. This book is a rallying cry and solid marching orders for postmodern Christians. We must all realize that God loves us very much. He knows what we're going through. He wants the best for us, and He has placed us here for a reason.

Clay Crosse

Acknowledgments

Thank you to:

- John Mark Yeats. The genesis for this project began the afternoon we sat in Schlotzsky's Deli discussing C.S. Lewis's *The Abolition of Man*. Thank you for helping to open my eyes to the real world.
- My daughters, Bethany, Hannah, and Sarah, who over the course of the past few years heard me go on and on and on about what was to become this book. Thank you for your patience.
- My wife, Valerie, for your constant encouragement and support. Without you, none of this would be worth doing.
- Mark Tobey and Elizabeth Newenhuyse of Moody Publishers for believing in this project and helping to make it a reality and to Ali Childers for her fine editorial work.

Part One
Welcome to Oz

*C*ome along, Toto," she said. "We will go to the Emerald City and ask the Great Oz how to get back to Kansas again."

I Have a Feeling We're Not in Kansas Anymore

Anne never could get used to the smell. An odd combination of smoke, animal feces, dust, and sweat, the odor hung in the air everywhere she went in this African village where her daughter and son-in-law lived. "About halfway through the trip, I thought I was going to lose it. I just couldn't take it any longer," she said. "Of course, no matter how much I complained nothing changed." Her daughter hardly noticed the smell. When Anne would say something about the odor, Jennifer would take a half-hearted sniff in the air and say something like, "Oh, you get used to it after a while."

Anne's husband, Leroy, hated the altitude. He had thought he was in decent enough shape for a fifty-year-old man. Then he stepped off the plane in Addis Ababa in the high plateau region of Africa. The elevation sucked the wind out of him. Every few minutes an aching in his chest forced him to stop to catch his breath. "I was ready to go home after about two days," he said.

Then there were the African children, each of whom seemed in desperate need of a tissue with which to blow his nose. "But," said Anne, "all the Kleenex in the world wouldn't have done any good. With so much dust blowing everywhere, I don't understand how anyone could ever breathe normally." A photo of the children with Anne shows them huddled around her, each one doing their best to hug her while others clung to her hands.

Anne and Leroy learned about their limitations during their two-week stay in Ethiopia. They discovered how American they truly are. Everything from the food to the language to the poverty of east Africa overwhelmed them. "I hoped we could work with Jennifer and Adrian while we were there. I thought there must be something we could do," Anne said. "But most of the time I felt like I was in the way. Almost everything I felt that I should do was wrong, from the way I talked to the people to the gifts I wanted to hand out. I thought I was being compassionate by giving candy to the children. Adrian told me I wasn't doing any of them any favors." She paused. "I thought I knew what to expect over there, but I didn't have a clue. It truly is a completely different world."

WHERE DID MY WORLD GO?

Anne and Leroy climbed aboard a 747 that became like a time machine, transporting them to a world that has barely changed over a thousand years. Another sort of time warp has changed your life and mine. Without climbing aboard an airplane, we've been transported to a different culture than the one in which we grew up. One morning we woke in a world not locked in the past, but in the future. No one is really sure what to call this place. Even the most popular categorization, postmodernism, says more about what this world *isn't* than what it is.

Nothing looks familiar here, and the moment we think that we have our bearings, the world changes again. Marketing expert George Barna has said that every three to five years this culture completely reinvents itself, with the process compressing with each passing cycle.[1] It appears that all of the foundations of the past have crumbled. In this strange new world, even the definition of the word *is* is in question.

The new world assaults our senses, especially our sense of right and wrong. Personal ethics are just that, personal. Most of the natives of this land gave up the concept of transcendent, eternal truth long ago. Like beauty, truth is in the eye of the beholder—a matter of taste, not absolutes. "Does it work for me?" is the question of the day, not "Is this right, ethical, or moral?" Being true to oneself is the highest good and ultimate virtue.

That's not all that makes us uncomfortable in this world. The people here—they seem different. Some of their ideas leave us baffled. Natives of this land value experience the way that earlier generations valued material wealth. Because of this, many people live in a state of perpetual boredom. We try to tell them that there's more to life than being entertained, but they don't listen. Most of us wonder if they listen to anyone. They aren't swayed by the opinion of experts. To the natives of this postmodern world, the experts might as well be dead.

Everything around us has changed. The new world swallowed our old world, leaving us dazed, confused, isolated—and most of us want to find a way home. We feel a little like Dorothy on the day when she stepped out of the scenery of the black-and-white farmhouse and entered the Technicolor world of Oz. If only we could click our heels and wake up in our own bed in our own little Kansas, we would feel much better. That's how Anne and Leroy felt during their two-week stay in the African bush. It was a nice place to visit, but . . .

Authenticity is the key to effectiveness in Oz.

Anne and Leroy could go home. We don't have that option. For those of us old enough to remember watching Neil Armstrong stepping down onto the lunar surface, that world where we grew up no longer exists. There is no going home.

Now what?

Either we can continue to be a stranger in a strange land, or we can adjust. We can whine and complain and wish that the good old days would return, or we can accept the fact that God knows what He is doing, roll up our sleeves, and carry on His work in this world and this culture that He has allowed to flourish.

The only real difference between Anne and Leroy and their daughter's family was a sense of call. Adrian and Jennifer didn't step off the airplane and find life in the bush a particularly pleasant experience. The poverty of the people, both materially and spiritually, broke their hearts. But leaving Africa has never been an option for Adrian and Jennifer. They committed themselves to making whatever adjustments necessary to become effective ambassadors of Christ to the people of Yasow because God called them there.

I don't know if I ever heard God call me to reach out to

natives of the postmodern culture. He did something much more subtle. Without my knowledge and without my consent, He planted me in the postmodern world. The new world is now my home, and yours. By sticking us here God gave us a job to do. Whether we like it or not, we're now ambassadors of Christ to this world. We are, in the truest sense of the word, on a mission to a postmodern Oz.

In the pages that follow we will explore this new world. We will look around at the landscape, get to know the people, and take the initial steps to learn the language. Don't worry if you feel a little overwhelmed and homesick. Culture shock hits all missionaries no matter where they serve. We not only have to learn how to understand the people around us, but we must also unlearn many of the presuppositions of the modern world that only handicap us in the postmodern world and beyond.

Understanding the culture is only the first step toward impacting it with eternal truth. As we try to come to grips with the change that surrounds us, we must move out of the safety of the familiar. Don't worry. It isn't as difficult as it may seem. All of us, regardless of our age, have been affected by the shift from modernity to postmodernity. There's a little postmodern in all of us. Reaching the natives of Oz isn't a matter of trying to be something you aren't. On the contrary: Authenticity is the key to effectiveness in Oz.

I don't know about you, but I'm excited about what is ahead. God is at work here. The massive shift in our culture didn't take Him by surprise. He has now placed you and me in a new world filled with new challenges and new possibilities. Once we recover from the initial shock, we will discover that there is no better place to fulfill His mission.

CHAPTER TWO

Riding the Cyclone

And now to address the obvious question: What is postmodernism? While the term may sound new and trendy, the word was first used back in the 1920s to describe a style of architecture. Later it crept into the art world, then into philosophy. Finally it became the vogue term to describe Western culture in the late twentieth and early twenty-first centuries. In Christian circles, the term emerged in the 1990s through books by such thinkers as Leonard Sweet and Stanley Grenz. The word has now been around long enough that seminars are being held to discuss what will come after postmodernism.

Some want to confine postmodernism to a single generation. They use the term the same way that people throw around expressions like *Baby Boomer* and *Buster* and *Gen-X, -Y,* and *-Z.* But trying to confine the effects of postmodernity to one group of people ignores the fact that this shift in history has affected us all. Therefore, when I refer to residents of Oz, I am referring to everyone alive during this postmodern moment in history.

We could say that postmodernism is nothing more than the age in which we live—the era that came after the modern age, but that doesn't really describe the phenomena that we see around us. The postmodern Oz is far more than a period of time. It encompasses more than a generation born between the Challenger and Colombia disasters. The concept moves beyond time or space or generations to encompass a unique way of comprehending reality. And (prepare to be a little confused) it refuses to be confined to one way of seeing the world, and yet, every worldview it spawns springs forth from the same basic assumptions about reality.

A WORLD WITHOUT A CENTER

So what is postmodernism? At its most basic level, it describes the world in which we find ourselves, a world without a center. To understand a world without a center, think in terms of a bicycle wheel. On the outside of the wheel sits a tire, which is attached to a rim, which is held in place by spokes, all of which are connected to a center axle. Cultures and societies are made up of more than people. They consist of laws and rules that are based upon underlying ethics and morals, which didn't arise in a vacuum. Like spokes connected to a center axle, the ethics and morals must be connected to something greater than themselves, something greater than the culture itself. To last, they must be connected to a transcendent center which not only serves as the basis for ethics and morals, but also forms the basic way of seeing and understanding the world for the people within this culture.

Between the fourth century (when Christianity became the official state religion of the Roman Empire) and the early seventeenth century, the majority of the Western world considered the church or a loose idea of God as the center of morality. A minority held to superstitious beliefs.

In the middle of the seventeenth century, about the time another in a series of long and bloody wars between England and France came to a close, a shift occurred. Instead of looking to God as the source for ultimate truth, people came to believe they could discover a center on their own by using nothing but reason. God wasn't removed from the picture altogether, but He was pushed to the perimeter. He came to be viewed as an almighty being who created the world, including the natural laws that governed the way it worked, then left it to run on its own. They believed that they could discover a firm basis for morals and ethics and meaning to life on their own through reason and logic, without any sort of special revelation from God.

Mankind would prove to be an insufficient source of truth, values, and ethics.

This period of time is known as the Enlightenment. Truth still rested in the center, yet it was natural truth revealed by the workings of an orderly universe. People came to see this as a wonderful alternative to the divisiveness of Christianity. Enlightenment thinkers emphasized the harmony and order of nature. They also emphasized personal autonomy, believing every individual could discover truth on his own through reason. Above all, this period was marked by a firm belief in progress. Societies marched forward toward bigger and better things. God still played a role in people's lives, but He was no longer in the center of the lives of individuals or Western culture as a whole. Mankind filled that place.

The Enlightenment ended when the French Revolution took Enlightenment thought to its logical conclusion, going so far as to enthrone reason as a goddess. It didn't take long for the Revolution to degenerate into a bloodbath around the guillotine. The principles upon which the Enlightenment was built could not restrain the worst in man. Mankind would prove to be an insufficient source of truth, values, and ethics. The center collapsed, and into the space left behind arose the first modern dictator, Napoleon Bonaparte. By the time Napoleon was defeated at Waterloo, the Enlightenment had ended and the modern world was born.

BIRTH OF THE MODERN

The modern world dawned with the coming of the Industrial Revolution. The Enlightenment ideal of being able to discover universal truth through reason alone no longer held water. And philosophy didn't offer much in its place. People still believed in God, but He was pushed further away to the realm of feelings and emotions. Clinging to God might help people make it through tough times, but religion made less and less difference in the real world. Increasingly the modern world turned to two alternatives for a new center. These were government and science.

The rise of Communism (along with Socialism, Fascism, and Nazism) ultimately came about through man trying to take God's place once and for all. The state became the "all and all." Morals and ethics were based on the "will of the people," which really meant the will of the person in charge. Communist rulers reshaped every aspect of society however they pleased, while imprisoning or killing those who stood in their way. It didn't take long for the leaders of Communist regimes to become paranoid butchers, leaving behind a wake of economic, environmental, and human destruction.

In the Western world, people began turning to science for answers to the tough questions. The universe came to be seen as a machine whose secrets were waiting to be discovered. Once science unlocked these mysteries, it could solve the problems that plagued the human race. The crowning achievement of science came on July 20, 1969, as Neil Armstrong stepped down onto the lunar surface. That same summer, Woodstock celebrated the notion that it was possible to forge a society of peace and love without God or any other help. Anything and everything seemed possible. Putting a man on the moon was a pinnacle for science, though its failure to conquer all would become clear soon enough. While Neil and Buzz walked around the Sea of Tranquility, race riots and the Vietnam War raged on planet Earth.

A major blow to science and the modern age came in January 1986. On a cloudless morning, the shuttle *Challenger* exploded. Science could not solve all our problems. Many cast a wary eye toward technology. The same scientific advances that could make our lives easier could just as easily destroy us. And, at any given moment, we aren't too sure which scenario might play out next.

WHAT FINAL ANSWER?

Postmodernism arose as people gave up hope of finding some final answer, some transcendent truth, which would give meaning to life and provide a firm foundation for morals and values. So they stopped looking. Everything just is. Optimism and the Enlightenment belief in progress has given way to skepticism and cynicism. Life just goes on. No one waits for someone to come down from a mountain with THE ANSWER for life. Instead most people decided they needed to carve out an answer for themselves. Irish poet W.B. Yeats said it best:

> *"Things fall apart; the centre cannot hold;*
> *Mere anarchy is loosed upon the earth."*[1]

This is the defining characteristic of Oz. It is a culture that believes it has tried everything, only to discover that nothing works. People no longer ask about THE meaning of life. Instead they hope to find a way to impart some meaning to their own lives, some way to make their own life have purpose. Faith in the center has given way to the hope that I can find something that will help me make sense of today. Yet what works today may not work tomorrow. The result looks a lot like anarchy—at least moral and ethical anarchy. Majority votes and opinion polls have taken the place of transcendent truth. Whatever is right is whatever most people think is right.

THIS IS BAD, RIGHT?

At this point, we usually start talking about how horrible this turn of events is from a biblical perspective. Yet what came before it wasn't exactly good. In fact, when you read through history, you see that every culture and society was inherently flawed because they all have one common denominator: imperfect human beings. The

Bible tells us that every person who has ever lived has sinned and fallen short of the glory of God (Romans 3:23). Sin entered the world in the Garden of Eden, when the first man and woman chose to rebel against God, not on August 1, 1981 (the day MTV premiered). And lost people always find a way to act like lost people. We shouldn't be surprised when they do. Nearly 1,950 years ago Paul wrote in 2 Timothy 3:1-5:

> In the last days there will be very difficult times. For people will love only themselves and their money. They will be boastful and proud, scoffing at God, disobedient to their parents, and ungrateful. They will consider nothing sacred. They will be unloving and unforgiving; they will slander others and have no self-control; they will be cruel and have no interest in what is good. They will betray their friends, be reckless, be puffed up with pride, and love pleasure rather than God. They will act as if they are religious, but they will reject the power that could make them godly.

Peter echoed Paul as he wrote, "First, I want to remind you that in the last days there will be scoffers who will laugh at the truth and do every evil thing they desire" (2 Peter 3:3).

But, Peter also said, "In the last days, God said, I will pour out my Spirit upon all people. Your sons and daughters will prophesy, your young men will see visions, and your old men will dream dreams" (Acts 2:17). God knew that these last days would be difficult. That's why He pours out His Spirit on each one who surrenders his life to His Son. He didn't give us the Holy Spirit so we could hide. Far from it. The Spirit indwells us believers in order that we might prophesy—that is, that we might speak truth to this generation with the life-giving words of Jesus.

Oz, like every other society created by fallen human beings, is permeated by the lasting effects of the fall of mankind. Much about this place will strike us as anti-biblical and offensive, just as missionaries to India find the Hindu religion and caste system anti-biblical and offensive. Yet to gain a hearing on the streets of New Delhi, you don't begin by telling the people what is wrong with their country. Instead, you must train your mind to understand the culture. It is the environment its people have grown up in, as well as the context in which you have been called to do ministry. As people's lives are transformed by the gospel, change will take place on both personal and cultural levels. In the meantime, missionaries to India must faithfully live and proclaim the message of Jesus to all people regardless of the circumstances in which they live. Missionaries to Oz have to do the same thing in this world without a center where we've been placed to make a difference.

CHAPTER THREE

One of Everything, Please

Half of my childhood was spent on the Little League ball fields next to the Dairy Queen in Moore, Oklahoma. Through the spring and summer I played baseball, and autumn was the time for football. All the games for both sports were on the same fields. The town moved the bleachers to correspond with either a baseball diamond or a one-hundred-yard rectangle so that our parents could watch. None of the fields had much grass; an overabundance of red clay and multiple ball games every night saw to that. One or two fields boasted a healthy population of goat-head thorns that got caught in one's pants, socks, and shoelaces. Those goat heads made the football games even more interesting. And baseballs always took funny bounces, since no matter how many times the town tried to smooth out the infields, they could never repair the damage inflicted during football season.

As bad as the fields were, all my friends and I loved

them for one reason: the concession stand. It was the only place on earth we knew of where we could get our favorite beverage. In fact, this beverage could be called the official soft drink of the Moore, Oklahoma, Little League sports universe in the 1960s and '70s. We all drank it. After every game, win or lose, our coaches lined us up and brought us to the concession stand for a free soda. Baseball or football, whether the weather was hot or cold, it didn't matter. We always got a free soda. And 90 percent of us ordered the same drink, the best concoction a nine-year-old boy can imagine. When our turn came to step up to the concession window, we all said the same thing: "Give me a Suicide."

I don't know who named this odd combination of tastes "the Suicide," but the name stuck. The Suicide consisted of one long squirt from every available soda flavor in the concession stand. Our variety consisted of one part Coke, one part root beer, one part 7-Up, and one part orange soda. I must have consumed ninety-three gallons of Suicides during my Little League football and baseball careers. Once or twice my friends and I tried to make our own, but they were never the same. No other place could capture the unique flavor that came from combining that soda fountain's Coke, root beer, 7-Up, and orange soda.

Of course, no one could appreciate the taste of a Suicide quite like a boy who had just spent the past two hours accumulating sticky burrs in his football pants. Our parents couldn't. Most usually groaned and said something like, "Don't you want something *normal* this time?" The teenage girl working the concession stand couldn't. My sisters couldn't. In their boring existences, they stuck with drinking one variety of soda at a time. No self-respecting, preteen male ballplayer could settle for just one kind of soda—not when you could have them all at the same time.

IN SEARCH OF A BIG STORY

Postmodern culture takes the same approach to the marketplace of ideas. Rather than choose one concept of right and wrong or one standard by which everyone must live, in our postmodern Oz, all worldviews are welcome. Every idea, no matter how odd it may sound, is not only tolerated but also warmly accepted. When it comes to what is normal or abnormal, people want both/and, not either/or. We're open to every possibility. Author and professor of social thought Allan Bloom observed: "Openness —and the relativism that makes it the only plausible stance in the face of various claims to truth and various ways of life and kinds of human beings—is the great insight of our time. *The true believer is the real danger* [emphasis added]."[1]

Some experts say that the defining characteristic of the age in which we live is the total rejection of absolute truth. While technically correct, it doesn't give the full picture of what is going on around us. As we saw in the last chapter, people reject the idea of a center or absolute truth, but that doesn't mean they do not believe that truth exists. Rather, they reject the notion that one concept of truth is adequate to explain everything. Whether the ideas come from science or the Bible or Buddhism or Mom or Dad, citizens of Oz have come to believe the universe in which we live is so big, so complex, and so beyond our ability to grasp, that no one explanation of how to make sense of it all will work. No big story can bring order to the universe. An "absolute truth" which supersedes all other truth cannot be found.

The modern world ended when people stopped looking for a single answer to the meaning of life. The discovery of a multiplicity of possible explanations has been liberating to the people of Oz. While they do not believe that one truth will work for all people for all times, they are more open to an ever-expanding variety of small explanations. Now, rather than have some expert tell them how they need to live or what they need to do for their lives to matter, everyone is free to choose his own path. People in Oz still believe in truth, but now truth is a very personal matter. They believe in what is true for them and whatever combination of ideas works to help them make it in life and achieve the highest goal in the Emerald City: happiness.

And they apply this approach to everything.

GOD OF THE SUICIDE

People in Oz apply the Suicide-soda approach to the idea of God. During the modern age, evolution and science told people God was dead. We were told that we are nothing more than the end result of a series of cosmic accidents that ultimately resulted in the human race. We are alone in the universe. No higher power is out there to help us make it through the cold vacuum of space. We heard this for decades, but no one totally bought it. Today, people realize their need for a belief in God more than ever before. Nine out of ten of the people in the United States believe in God. The numbers hold true across the spectrum of ages. Books on spirituality top the best-seller charts, while God plays an ever-expanding role in prime-time television shows and movies. Daytime talk show hosts devote large segments of time to discussing topics like "remembering your spirit," where the viewer is encouraged to get in touch with his spiritual side. People long to connect with something beyond themselves, some power greater than the limitations of being human. They want God.

Belief in God may be soaring, but attendance in churches has decreased over the past couple of decades. People of Oz may want God, but they don't want traditional religion. In its place, people in the postmodern world take all sorts of ideas about gods and deities and combine them to make their own customized lord. They don't want to have to choose between being a Christian or a Buddhist. Instead they choose both. A few years ago one of the most decorated Olympic athletes of all time released his autobiography. In one chapter he gave his testimony of how he accepted Jesus as his Lord and Savior. A few pages later he talked about his New Age guru who helped connect him with the positive forces of the universe. A later chapter told of his sexual exploits. And, apparently, neither he nor many of his readers saw any contradictions between these ideas. They all worked together for him. He'd found truth, his truth, just the way he liked it.

If everything is true, then nothing is true

A SUICIDE MORALITY

Questions of morality fall into the same mix of ideas. In this culture, every concept of what constitutes moral behavior is equally valid. When asked, people will say they do not believe in absolute moral truth, not because they do not believe in morality, but because they believe no one set of teachings can define morality for everyone. Ultimately, they say, each of us has to choose what is moral for us. Truth is a question of preference and taste. I have to be true to myself and do what I believe to be the right thing. My right thing may not be right for you, nor may it even be right for me in a different situation, but that's not the point. I must choose from all I've heard about right and wrong to select what will ultimately work best for me.

Postmodern culture takes the same approach to ideas about what it means to be a male or a female. Traditionally, people had a pretty good idea of what it meant to be a man or a woman. Not any more. Many residents of Oz haven't just rejected traditional roles. Instead they regard gender and sexual identities as nothing more than labels. Male, female, heterosexual, homosexual, bisexual—these are not identities, but they are roles a person plays. In Oz, you can be whatever you want to be. Julie from Philly, answering a question on the Web site of the AIDS activist group ACT UP, said it best, "I am a bisexual woman who in the past has identified as lesbian while today has a boyfriend. I can be sometimes one thing and sometimes something else—that's the nice thing about fluid postmodern sexuality."[2]

CHOICE AS ULTIMATE TRUTH

In Oz, every issue comes down to my own personal choice. No one needs experts because experts want to impose one set of ideas on everyone. People in Oz don't want one set of ideas. They want them all. That's why many come home from the doctor's office and immediately begin surfing the Internet. A doctor may tell them their gall bladder doesn't work and that it needs to come out, but they can't stop there. They want to hear all the options from every source, traditional and nontraditional. And after they've heard from everybody they will decide what course of action they need to take. It's not that they don't think the doctor knows what he is talking about. He does. But he is also just one voice. When they step up to the concession stand of truth they order "the Suicide" whether the subject is god or medicine or morality or how to raise a ferret.

Of course, in the end, trying to choose everything ends up being a choice for nothing. If everything is true, then nothing is true. The only way to call every available option of ideas equally valid, even when they contradict one another, is to understand deep down that none of them are real. We can draw pictures of Santa Claus rendering him black or white, skinny or fat, dressed in red or green, bearded or clean shaven, and all of them work because no one lives in a toy factory at the North Pole. But if he did slide down my chimney one Christmas Eve all of my ideas about him would have to conform to the real person eating milk and cookies by the fireplace. Until he shows up, I am free to do with him whatever I like.

The postmodern Oz tolerates every idea of right and wrong, truth and lie, normal and abnormal, only because it does not believe any one absolute standard exists. And if one absolute standard does not exist, every other standard is equally true because they are all equally false. All are nothing more than manmade illusions with no basis in fact. Deep down, people in this land are convinced nothing is real, nothing is true, and nothing matters. Even still, they embrace everything, behaving as though their personal preferences of truth validate themselves.

WHEN REALITY COMES KNOCKING

I stopped drinking Suicides sometime around my twelfth birthday. I can't remember the exact day, but I do remember thinking as I drained my last one, "This tastes disgusting." And it did. Suicides never caught on in mass culture because their repulsive brown color and super-sweet, indistinguishable taste made most people sick to their stomachs. But during my Little League sports career, neither my friends nor I wanted to admit what we knew to be true. We knew the Suicide was horrid, but that didn't stop us from ordering them. Our preference was really an illusion, one we didn't dare destroy in the presence of our friends.

In the same way, postmodern Oz is built on the illusion that I can make sense of my world and my life by accepting every idea, no matter how strange and no matter how contradictory. But in the end it doesn't work. In an attempt to have everything, I end up with nothing. And nothing is a hard thing to build a life on.

CHAPTER FOUR

Strawberry Fields Lie Just to the Left of the Yellow Brick Road

The Luftwaffe pilot made a quick pass over the harbor near Kent, England. His camera snapped off a few pictures before making a quick turn east to avoid antiaircraft fire. As his plane started back across the English Channel toward occupied France, he looked back at the scene below him. Landing craft filled the harbor, and he could see tents and tanks further west. The invasion force grew larger every week.

"It won't be much longer," he thought to himself, "before the First U.S. Army storms across the channel toward Pas-de-Calais." A chill ran down his spine as a shell exploded just to the right of his plane. He raced to the safety of the open water.

Every reconnaissance flight confirmed what the German commanders had suspected for months. The Allied forces would execute their long-anticipated, amphibious invasion of France at Pas-de-Calais. Now the only question was when.

Hitler, himself, first came to the conclusion that Pas-de-Calais would be the invasion point. He concentrated some of his best Panzer tank divisions in that region and ordered the construction of permanent defenses of steel-reinforced concrete around its perimeter. In the spring of 1944, Allied bombing intensified along the coast of France, with much of the bombing focusing on Calais. This only strengthened their suspicions about where the D-Day invasion would begin. Somehow, area radar facilities escaped harm, allowing the Fifteenth Panzer division to see any attack force long before they would arrive. Also in early 1944, came the news that George S. Patton had been given command of the First Army amassing near Kent, England, not far from Dover. German military leaders respected Patton as the greatest Allied commander. If an invasion was to come, he surely would be the man to lead it.

On the morning of June 6, 1944, German radar screens in this area lit up. Blips signifying an unbelievable number of ships filled their screens. Troops went on a state of high alert. Crews manning the cannons in the concrete Atlantic-wall defense system ran to their posts. In the meantime, news began to filter in from the south that eight other Allied divisions had launched an invasion near Normandy, which only increased the tension in Pas-de-Calais. The Normandy invasion was surely a ruse meant to distract the Nazis and pull troops and tanks away from the Allies' primary objective.

But the ships on the radar screens never appeared on the horizon of Pas-de-Calais. Apparently they had turned back to wait for more favorable weather. Meanwhile to the south, the Normandy invasion was going poorly for the German Wehrmacht. In spite of massive casualties on both sides, the Germans had lost the beaches of Normandy by the end of the day, and the invasion of France and ultimately Germany had begun. Still, the German Fifteenth Army and the other troops in and around Calais continued to wait for the "real" invasion, an invasion that never came.

Patton's First Army didn't storm across the English Channel toward Pas-de-Calais, because that army did not exist. The tanks, armored personnel carriers, and transport ships that Luftwaffe reconnaissance aircraft had photographed for months were nothing more than giant balloons. German spies in England, who sent reports to the fuhrer of massive troop buildups, were sending false intelligence. Every one of the spies had been captured by the British and were either imprisoned or forced to become double agents. Even the radar images of ships proved false, created by Allied planes dropping pieces of foil across the channel along the path ships would take if a real invasion had occurred. Allied bombers had spared the radar sites precisely for this moment. For weeks the Germans didn't realize they'd been duped. By the time they finally released their tanks and troops from Calais, the Allied armies were marching into Paris. By feeding the Nazis a false reality, the Allied commanders saved thousands upon thousands of lives during the real invasion on D-Day in Normandy and hastened the end of the war.

MAYBERRY AND VIETNAM

People in Oz are undergoing a similar deception, yet they aren't entirely victims. The line between what is real and what isn't has become incredibly blurred. In this place you could well say that nothing is real, or at least no one really knows what is real. It's not just that people cannot tell the difference between fantasy and reality. Many do not want to know the difference. There's both an element of deception and self-delusion where what is real is steadily replaced by what postmodern philosophers call *hyper-reality.*

One of the most influential voices of postmodernism, French philosopher Jean Baudrillard, maintained that this state of flux between fantasy and reality was inevitable in a media-saturated world. He likened the constant flow of images that invade our lives through television and movies and the Internet to a vampire sucking the life out of us.[1] We lose the ability to discern what is real and what isn't. But the idea of hyper-reality goes beyond this sort of confusion. True hyper-reality comes as the images and models of reality become more real than the real world itself.

I know this concept seems like it comes straight out of left field, but most of us have been affected by it to one degree or another. And my favorite television show is one of the culprits. Most days I eat lunch with Andy, Barney, Opie, Otis, and all the other good people of Mayberry. I down a plate of angel hair pasta covered with balsamic vinegar and parmesan cheese while watching the sheriff without a gun and his Wyatt-Earp-of-a-deputy foil bank robbers or try to convince Helen and Thelma Lou that they really don't want to date the fun girls. I've seen every episode countless times, but I still watch because it is one of the best shows ever made.

The Andy Griffith Show and other black-and-white television comedies from the golden age of television convey the image that America was once simpler, more honest, and more wholesome than the new millennium. Andy didn't wear a gun, and most of us think of those days as a time when people didn't have to lock their doors and violence didn't fill the streets. But the world of Mayberry never existed. *The Andy Griffith Show* was filmed during the 1960s, one of the most explosive periods in American history. The show is completely devoid of any references to the struggle for civil rights or the antiwar movement. How else could Gomer Pyle enlist in the Marine Corps and not worry about fighting in Southeast Asia? In this show there are no drugs, no "free love," and none of the social unrest of the decade. The only social problem is alcohol, and even then no one drinks but Otis.

This is hyper-reality, where our ideas of the '50s and early '60s come from heavily censored images produced for television. And in many minds, these electronic images have become more real than what actually happened during this period of American history.

We don't have to go back to the black-and-white world of Andy and *I Love Lucy* to have hyper-reality intrude on our world. During both Gulf Wars, news networks fed us a constant diet of sights and sounds from the Persian Gulf. We watched as smart bombs destroyed bridges and Patriot missiles shot down Scuds during the first conflict. And we witnessed the crowds tearing down statues of Saddam Hussein during the second war in Iraq. It was as though we were there. We know what happened. We saw it with our own eyes.

Yet the relationship between what we believed happened and the reality of war is fuzzy at best. All of our news comes to us the same way, heavily edited, portraying a small part of the actual events. Viewers at home are spared most of the gruesome details. Just as photographers at D-Day avoided filming bodies of American soldiers bouncing in the tide at Omaha Beach, the cameras in present-day conflicts do not show us the full horrors of war.

Postmoderns create a new reality when their old reality doesn't fit their expectations.

For that we have to go to the video stores to pick up a copy of *Saving Private Ryan* or *Three Kings*. This is the irony of Oz. Movies made about war show more realistic images than the actual footage of the conflicts, yet we know the movies aren't real. Or are they? That's hyper-reality. Professor Stanley Grenz believes this interweaving of fantasy and reality causes us to "look at the world in the same way we look at films, suspicious that what we see around us may in fact be illusion."[2]

THE LURE OF "REALITY"

The blurring of the line between fantasy and reality changes the way people in Oz see the world and themselves. They've grown very skeptical and suspicious of almost everything. People wonder if every bit of news is nothing but a ruse, and they smell conspiracies everywhere. That's why Web sites are devoted to exposing Neil Armstrong's moon walk as a hoax, and others claim the government was behind the 1995 Murrah Federal Building bombing in Oklahoma City. Every fact is doubted because the very definition of a fact is in doubt.

Faced with this kind of world, people in Oz also use hyper-reality as a way to create a world where they can find happiness. Postmoderns create a new reality when their old reality doesn't fit their expectations. And the lure of the new realities can be very strong. This afternoon I opened the newest copy of my favorite weekly sports magazine. There was an advertisement for a calendar featuring women in swimsuits. These women do not look like 98 percent of the women who live on planet Earth. They were much thinner, yet had larger breasts, and their skin didn't have a single blemish. These are the models of the "perfect" female. But they aren't real. The models that fill the pages of magazines have been reshaped by surgeons, extreme dieting, exercise that most people don't have time for, and to top it off, their photographs are enhanced to remove any imperfections. Some models are even made thinner by a photo computer program. This is hyper-reality, yet these pictures are supposed to portray the ultimate female.

SO WHAT DOES THIS MEAN?

As the copies of reality become their own reality, the real world begins to look less and less real. It's not just that people prefer an artificial world to the third planet from the sun. The fuzziness between fantasy and reality adds to the disorientation that is caused by the loss of a center and the absence of absolute truth. In the last two chapters, we traced the progression from a world centered on faith and superstition to a world centered on man and reason, to the modern world, which placed its faith in man and science. The postmodern world isn't centered on anything. It gave up the hope of finding any one answer big enough to explain the intricacies of human existence. While residents of Oz are more open than ever to everything offered in the marketplace of ideas (even when those ideas contradict one another), deep down they believe that every concept of truth is inherently flawed. All truth is acceptable, because no truth is true.

Which brings us back to the very idea of reality. In Oz, truth is just one more piece of hyper-reality. All the ideas for why we are here, the explanations of what constitutes normal or abnormal, and all the rules that give order to society have come to be viewed as just one more human creation. These rules and explanations have meaning only because we give them meaning. Everything is thus in doubt. Everything can be ignored or reshaped to fit my personal tastes. As if that isn't confusing enough, postmodern thinkers have applied this to every part of human existence, including the words we use. They say that all language is merely a grid placed upon reality in an attempt to reduce it down to an understandable size. To them, all words are little more than meaningless noise to which we have assigned artificial meaning. In short, nothing is real.

THE REAL QUESTION

If this makes your head hurt, join the club. Yet if we want to reach out to postmoderns, we need to understand how they see the world and the kinds of questions that they ask. No one in Oz asks what is true. What is *real* is the question. The people who live here have grown weary of the constant bombardment of false realities. They're tired of being lied to and being told what is good for them when it has no basis in fact. They long for something permanent, something genuine, something that looks even better once the wrapping has been stripped away. That is why spirituality is more popular than ever, even as Christianity continues to lose ground. But here is the real paradox: By longing for something real, people in Oz seek something that deep down they do not believe exists. That leaves them more than a little confused, not knowing where to look.

The inability of the German military to distinguish between fantasy and reality on the eve of D-Day hastened their destruction. As the line between reality and hyper-reality grows fuzzier and fuzzier in Oz, the urgency of our mission becomes clearer. People are asking what is real. How we respond to that question will impact not only individual lives, but also the long-term survival of our society as a whole.

CHAPTER FIVE

Hands-on and High-Touch

Greg liked to jump out of airplanes. He jumped by himself, and he jumped with groups. He jumped with cameras strapped to his head, and he jumped with novices strapped to his back. He performed loops and rolls and stacks where he and other jumpers lined their parachutes up on top of one another. When he started dating his wife, he talked her into jumping out of airplanes with him. It was a prerequisite for a long-term relationship. Greg even gained a bit of media attention from jumping out of airplanes. Some of the video he shot in the air played on national television on *Real Videos* and *America's Funniest Home Videos*. But Greg didn't jump out of airplanes to end up on television. He jumped because he loved the experience of falling through the air and floating back to earth.

Greg doesn't jump out of airplanes anymore. He quit the day he that realized that nothing about skydiving scared him. A skydiver without fear is a skydiver headed for a serious accident, so Greg quit that hobby. These days he finds excitement by riding along with his police officer friend on his night patrols, rafting down some of the world's toughest white-water rapids, and speeding down the highway at 165 miles per hour on a motorcycle. Greg might sound crazy, but he isn't. He lives in Oz, and like the people around him, he just wants to experience life close-up and hands-on.

They will go anyplace, try anything, and pay any amount to feel fully alive.

People in Oz want to experience all that life can be—to immerse themselves in it and feel a rush of adrenaline and a pounding heartbeat. They may never go so far as to leap out of a plane or speed down the interstate at 165 miles per hour, but they will go anyplace, try anything, and pay any amount to feel fully alive. The experience is worth the price of admission.

"COME INTO MY STORE"

Courtney discovered a new shopping experience while walking down the streets of Cozumel, Mexico, during a family vacation. "Senorita, senorita," the voices called out to her as she strolled past the open-air shops, "Come into my store and see what I have. I have many nice things. Come and see." Courtney ignored the first few. When she walks through the mall near her house, the salespeople from the Gap don't usually call out from the entryway of their store. But eventually something caught her eye, and Courtney stepped into the dimly lit shop and into a whole new world.

Nothing in the store had a price tag, which struck her as a little odd. "How much for this one?" Courtney asked, holding up a solid silver bracelet. The shopkeeper took the bracelet, held it up to catch a better look at it, then weighed it on a small scale next to the cash register. "Forty dollars American," he replied. Courtney shrugged her shoulders, put the bracelet down and started to move on to the next store. "Wait," the man said after she'd only taken three or four steps. "If you like the bracelet I can let you have it for thirty dollars."

Courtney smiled. "That's okay," she said. "I'll keep looking."

"Twenty-five," he replied. "Here, try it on, see how it looks on your wrist." Courtney turned around and walked back into the store. "Fifteen," she said. In that moment she discovered the fine art of haggling—and a fuller shopping experience. Now Courtney refuses to pay full price for anything. And no one calls to her from the door of her new favorite store, but perhaps that's because it doesn't have a door. Through *eBay* she gets to experience the same thrill she first felt on the streets of the Mexican island. "I know with *eBay* I often end up paying more than I would other places, but that doesn't matter," Courtney said. "Once you get in, it stops being about the merchandise." The hunt, the haggling, the contest to gain the upper hand and win a bargain—it's all there. And she's hooked.

Courtney isn't alone. An average of sixty-nine million users spend $59 million a day on everything from Beanie Babies to BMWs in the one-on-one Internet auction site.[1] It's more than a place to find bargains. It has become the open-air shop of Oz where the owner beckons you to come and see his wares. It's more than shopping. It's an experience. And people can't get enough of it.

BEYOND SPECTATOR SPORTS

Tony never played in the big leagues, but he loves the game. When Mark McGwire chased down Roger Maris throughout the 1998 season, Tony was there. He made several trips to St. Louis just to watch "Big Mac" make history. But Tony does more than watch the game. He manages his own team. None of his players know they're playing for Tony, since he never walks into a dugout or hands a line-up card to the umpire at home plate.

> Everything has to be hands-on, high-touch, high-participation.

That didn't stop him from staying up until three in the morning the night he drafted his fantasy baseball team. Tony competes via the Internet against a group of friends spread across the country. He does this every season because he loves the game.

Tony isn't some sports or computer geek who needs to get a life. Far from it. Through the magic of his fantasy baseball, Tony has moved from being an observer of baseball to being a participant. His team allows him to experience the game beyond the stands and beyond television. That's how Tony wants his baseball served up. Don't just show him the game or tell him who won in a box score. Tony lives in Oz, and people in Oz want the full baseball experience, the thrill of victory and the agony of defeat.

And if Tony's beloved Cardinals happen to win the World Series, all the better.

YOU BE THE STAR

Some cultures value truth. Others chase gold. In the postmodern world, the greatest commodity is experience. Author and futurist Leonard Sweet put it this way:

> *Experience is the currency of postmodern economics. . . .*
> *Moderns want to figure out what life's about. Postmoderns*
> *want to experience what life is, especially experience life for*
> *themselves. Postmoderns are not willing to live at arm's*
> *length distance from experience. They want life to explode*
> *all around them.*[2]

The desire for new and better experiences touches every part of life in Oz. From education to economics to entertainment, we've moved from an emphasis on information to immersion in the thing itself. Everything has to be hands-on, high-touch, high-participation.

The people who make commercials understand this. In the early days of car advertisements, ad companies dispensed information about their product. They emphasized engine size and carburetion and safety ratings and tire pressure and all sorts of mundane information in small print that filled half the page. After the oil crisis of the early '70s, television commercials featured gas mileage statistics in huge letters that covered the screen. Not anymore. Advertisers no longer try to sell cars; they peddle the driving experience. My favorite is the SUV ad where a man kayaking off the Pacific coast uses his car as a foghorn. Outside of the guy in the ad, no one who ever buys the car will use it as a foghorn while kayaking off the rocky coast of California, but that is irrelevant. These days, we're buying experience.

And we don't want to confine ourselves to watching television. We want to participate in it. The first reality television show was born when Allen Funt took his camera outside of the studio and placed it in the middle of everyday life. He called the results *Candid Camera*. Since then, some type of reality TV has always been on the air, with shows like *Real People* and *That's Incredible!* and the ever-popular *America's Funniest Home Videos*. Yet reality television as a medium didn't take off until producers made the person sitting in their living room a vital part of the action. *American Idol* and *Cupid* and whatever programs will follow in their wake aren't just reality television. They are participatory television. The viewer doesn't watch from afar; she shapes the show and determines what direction it will take. That's what postmoderns want. If they can't participate firsthand in the show itself, they want programs that will allow them to try the action on their own. A disclaimer popping up on the screen saying "Don't try this at home" simply means they should probably go to a friend's house to try jumping over cakes in a shopping cart.

MATH YOU CAN TOUCH

The taste and touch and feel world has also invaded the classroom. Jenny didn't learn math the way she now teaches it. She learned the old way where students memorized formulas by rote and worked out problems longhand. Her students' parents learned math that way, as did their parents before them. That's why more than a few of them were taken aback when Jenny's students came home with a note requesting a pie for her class. Pie charts they expected. An actual pie was a surprise.

Jenny's math teachers never sliced a pie in class, but that's how her students are learning math. They still hear the old formulas, and they still have to add and subtract and multiply and divide on paper. Math wouldn't be math without solving problems with a pencil and paper. But Jenny doesn't stop there. Her students experience math. One-sixth becomes more than a *1* on a line with a *6* resting below it. When Jenny's class talks about one-sixth, they slice a pie into six pieces and start eating. They see one-sixth and touch one-sixth and smell one-sixth and taste one-sixth. Learning involves more than transferring information from one mind to another. Jenny teaches in Oz, and no one learns anything in Oz until they experience it.

WHY EXPERIENCE MATTERS

Living in Oz means letting life surround, cover, move, and make us. This affects all our choices, whether about cars, television programs, or learning styles. No one stops to think about why experiences are so important, any more than they stop to think about why they should breathe or eat or drink water. The longing for experience is simply a priority, and it permeates every aspect of life.

Residents of Oz may not stop and wonder why experience is the new commodity, but we should. Several factors contributed to getting us here. The first is economic. Since the end of the Second World War, the Western world has experienced unprecedented economic growth. While the economy nearly ground to a halt in the late '70s and early

'80s, prosperity came back with a vengeance after that. More disposable income means greater freedom to do things that other generations never dreamed of doing. Families travel more than past generations. They see and taste and experience places and cultures that our grandparents could only read about in books.

Economic factors only explain why postmoderns can pursue a wide variety of experiences. It doesn't tell us what would motivate restaurants to become miniature theme parks and specialty stores to sell lifestyles more than products. The answer lies in what we've already discovered regarding truth and reality and living in a world without a center. With nothing to anchor a life upon, people are left wandering around in the dark, searching for something, anything, that will make them feel alive. Since the rise of relativism and the loss of faith in a transcendent God, we've been told life doesn't have any purpose or meaning. Yet no one can live that way. Deep down inside every human being, regardless of the age in which he lives, there is a longing to make sense of life and make it count beyond our earthly existence.

After being told we can't look to the heavens for the answer, and discovering through the failure of the Enlightenment and the modern-age we can't look inside ourselves for the answer, we finally started looking around. Experience has become more than a means of entertainment, selling cars, and learning math. Experiencing life has become the path whereby life has meaning. It is the way people in Oz feel truly alive.

This should be good news to us as we reach out to Oz. Many of our methods of telling people about Christ are stuck in the modern world. We think if we can disperse adequate information, people will be convinced Jesus is the way, the truth, and the life, and turn to Him. Those methods don't work any longer. I'm not sure they ever did. People aren't looking for information about God. They want to experience God, Himself. Information leaves them bored, uninterested. Experience, especially the ultimate experience any human being can ever have, leaves them breathless. And that's exactly what we have to offer.

CHAPTER SIX

"I Saw the Potato"

When Coca-Cola entered the mainland Chinese market in the 1920s, the company didn't know what to call their product. They knew choosing Mandarin characters that phonetically matched *ko-ka-ko-la* might result in some nonsensical or embarrassing phrase. No one in their Atlanta headquarters wanted to take that chance. But they also didn't want to delay filling shelves across China with the "Real Thing" while they sifted through the forty thousand characters that make up the Chinese alphabet, looking for the perfect name. As the old saying goes, money talks, so the company decided not to. They introduced Coca-Cola without giving it a Chinese name as they continued to look for an alternative.

But it is hard to sell a nameless product, and a bottle covered with English letters doesn't speak to a Mandarin-speaking country. The corporate guys back in the United States might have been able to take their time trying to come up with the perfect combination of four Chinese characters, but the people trying to peddle a new soft drink on the street couldn't. Chinese shopkeepers took matters into their own hands and picked four letters that sounded like the English name Coca-Cola. They put the name on signs all over the marketplace. It was a hit in China. Thirsty shoppers loved it, although more than one wondered why anyone would call a carbonated beverage "Bite the wax tadpole."

Coca-Cola wasn't the only product to have a translation problem in China. Pepsi's catch phrase from the Sixties, "Come alive with the Pepsi generation," came across as "Pepsi brings your ancestors back from the dead." Chinese Stephen King fans probably loved it. Kentucky Fried Chicken didn't do much better. Their slogan "finger lickin' good" was translated "Eat your fingers off." Apparently eating KFC in China makes you hungry for more than chicken.

Big businesses aren't the only ones that found that their products lost a little something in translation. When the Pope visited Miami in the '80s, one local entrepreneur decided to make some money the old fashioned way—selling T-shirts. He had a few hundred shirts printed up, shirts that were supposed to say in Spanish "I saw the Pope." Unfortunately, he didn't speak Spanish, and he didn't check with anyone who did before he sent his design to the printers. Instead of selling "I saw the Pope" shirts, he ended up hawking "I saw the potato" shirts. If he had lived in Idaho, he might have broken even.

INFORMATION VERSES IMAGE

When Christians try to communicate their faith in Jesus Christ to a postmodern world, we often end up say-

ing something akin to "I saw the potato" without realiz-
ing it. Most people in America speak English whether they
consider themselves postmodern or not. English words
may fall from our lips as we tell others in Oz about Jesus
Christ, but we might as well be selling "Bite the wax tadpole" in a bottle. Our words make just as much sense.

The problem lies in the way we use the language. We
may live in a postmodern world, but when it comes to
talk about Jesus and the Bible and believing in God, our
persuasion is very modern. The modern world elevated
science, logic, and reason. We learned to break things
down into their smallest components using reason and
then form conclusions about meaning. That's why we dis-
sected frogs in biology and why preachers dissect Bible
verses in sermons. Meaning and truth lead to proof which
leads to belief. We believe because the evidence for Christ
demands a verdict. When all the facts are known, believing in Jesus makes sense—it is the only reasonable choice
any thinking person can make.

No one in Oz thinks like this. When people don't believe in the existence of absolute truth, then our appeals to
logic and reason won't make any sense. But that's only the
beginning. The words we use reflect the way our brains
are wired. And in the postmodern world, most people's
brains are wired for pictures, not information. Trying to
communicate using nothing but information in a land
where people communicate by sharing images is like
telling people to eat their fingers. No one understands
what we're trying to say because they can't see it.

That was the problem Marcia Clark and the other Los
Angeles County prosecutors faced in the most famous
trial of the '90s. Clark and her associates had the unenvi-
able task of trying to prove that one of the most popular

American athletes was a cold-blooded, double murderer. The case seemed like a slam dunk. National polls showed an overwhelming majority of Americans assumed O. J. Simpson was guilty, especially after watching him run from police on national television during the infamous white Bronco chase. Then there were the notes he wrote. And the bloody footprint. And the bloody glove. All the evidence appeared to point toward one inevitable conclusion: the Hall of Fame running back must be guilty.

During the trial the prosecution team poured on the information. They brought in witnesses and forensic experts and psychologists as they built their case. The evidence was clear, they said. O. J. did it. The defense used a different tactic. The centerpiece of their defense wasn't information, but an image of O. J. Simpson trying on the bloody gloves. The defense lawyer Johnnie Cochrane said over and over again, "If the gloves don't fit, you must acquit." The gloves didn't and the jury did. They found O. J. "not guilty" of all charges. Images, not evidence or information, carried the day.

LEARNING TO SPEAK THE LANGUAGE

Missionaries who pack up their belongings and move to the other side of the world can do one of two things. They can wait for the people they're trying to reach to learn English so they understand the gospel in our language, or the missionaries can learn the people's native language. You and I face the same choice if we're going to be missionaries in a postmodern Oz. We can wait for everyone who lives here to revert to information-based learning, or we can learn their language. I think the choice we have to make is obvious.

People in the postmodern world think in terms of images, and they communicate using stories. A steady stream of information makes their eyelids heavy and causes their minds to wander. But tell them stories of real people in the real world, and you have their undivided attention. When I went to high school, history was always the most boring subject of all. Too many dates. Too many places. Too much information. Yet Stephen Ambrose wrote history books that consistently topped the best-seller lists. How? He didn't rattle off statistics from the Second World War. Instead he told stories about the men and women who served there. He planted his readers in foxholes as planes dropped bombs over their heads. History might be boring, but the real stories of young men trying to stay alive as a nightmare unfolded around them captivated readers.

Ambrose spoke the language of the postmodern era. He told stories. And he created pictures with his words. Postmoderns love pictures. Home computer sales took off when users stopped having to learn strange computer languages like Fortran and MS-DOS and could instead point a little arrow at a picture on the screen to start a program. When I was a pastor, I found my sermons improved 1,000 percent in the minds of my parishioners when the church bought a video projector and I started using pictures and movies as illustrations. My thoughts didn't suddenly become more profound, but images flashing on a screen communicated my ideas better than the avalanche of words spilling from my mouth. Postmoderns speak the language of pictures, and when I learned to use this language, I connected with my audience.

ANCIENT FUTURE

The postmodern world isn't the first society to speak the language of stories and pictures. In a very real sense, the shift from the modern world to the postmodern world brought us back to our natural human dialect. Before anyone learned how to write down the history of his people, the stories traveled orally from generation to generation. The earliest forms of writing used pictures in place of letters. As writing progressed and alphabets formed, people wrote down the stories they'd passed down.

Learning to speak the language of the postmodern world isn't about learning something new, but something old. More than anything, it is a process of unlearning the trappings of an information-overloaded, modern mindset. When I first learned how to share my faith in Christ, I went through a course that taught us to use the acrostic GOGO. I started off talking about God's purpose for our lives, followed by explaining our need for a Savior. The second G stood for God's provision, which is Jesus, and the last O was our response, which meant turning from sin and placing one's faith in Christ. I memorized the whole presentation and all the supporting Bible verses and can still recite the script twenty years later. When I was a pastor, I encouraged people to use little booklets that contained essentially the same information. These booklets usually had names like

> The Bible already speaks the language of Oz with its story, mystery, and images.

"Steps to Peace with God," and "How to Have a Full and Meaningful Life."

Now I find myself standing back and asking if either of these reflects the way the Bible communicates the message of Jesus and God's desire to reconcile people to Himself. And my honest answer is no. God chose to write the Bible as a story. It doesn't dispense information about God; it tells His story over the course of sixty-six books and thousands of years. Jesus didn't hand out tracts or articulate steps to God through spiritual laws or handy acrostics. Instead He told stories, such as one about a farmer planting his seeds and another about a man waiting for his rebellious son to come home. When you step back after reading the Bible, you find certain images indelibly stamped on your brain. You see a manger in a barn and a man hanging on a cross and an empty tomb.

The Bible already speaks the language of Oz with its story, mystery, and images. Our greatest need is to learn to speak it as well. What is standing between the postmodern world and the living God is a people who forgot how to think and speak like the Book that we say directs our lives.

Part Two

A Brain, A Heart, Da' Nerve

*T*hen Oz asked, "What do you wish me to do?"

"Send me back to Kansas, where my Aunt Em and Uncle Henry are," she answered earnestly. "I don't like your country, although it is so beautiful. And I am sure Aunt Em will be dreadfully worried over my being away so long."

The eyes winked three times, and then they turned up to the ceiling and down to the floor and rolled around so queerly that they seemed to see every part of the room. And at last they looked at Dorothy again.

"Why should I do this for you?" asked Oz.

"Because you are strong and I am weak; because you are a Great Wizard and I am only a little girl."

"But you were strong enough to kill the Wicked Witch of the East," said Oz.

"That just happened," returned Dorothy simply; "I could not help it."

"Well," said the Head, "I will give you my answer. You have no right to expect me to send you back to Kansas unless you do something for me in return. In this country everyone must pay for everything he gets. If you wish me to use my magic power to send you home again you must do something for me first. Help me and I will help you."

"What must I do?" asked the girl.

"Kill the Wicked Witch of the West," answered Oz.

"But I cannot!" exclaimed Dorothy, greatly surprised.

CHAPTER SEVEN

Pay No Attention to that Man Behind the Curtain

The Wizard of Oz had it made. All the citizens of the Emerald City trembled at the thought of him. Everyone believed him to be all-powerful, yet fear kept anyone from asking him to do a thing. On the odd chance that someone stumbled into his palace, he'd constructed a floating head with bellowing fire that would boom, "I am Oz, the Great and Terrible." The sight sent most intruders running for their lives. Everyone revered him as a god, the builder and protector of the Emerald City.

But holding down the job as Oz the Terrible wasn't as easy as it might seem. The wizard had to keep the people cowering in fear because he knew the truth about himself. He was a humbug. A fake. A phony. In truth he had no more power than any other cheap circus act, which is what he was before a runaway balloon carried him to the land of Oz. When people saw him come down from the sky, they assumed him to be next to divine, and he was too afraid to tell them any different. Since he had nothing better to do, he convinced the people to build a palace and a great city in his honor. The city itself wasn't green, at least not in L. Frank Baum's original telling of the story of Dorothy's search for a way back to Kansas. The wizard only made it appear to be made of emeralds by coercing everyone into wearing green glasses.

It was a great life for the wizard as long as people believed the false reality he constructed and fell for the illusion of power projected by the floating head in the palace. The day Dorothy and her friends walked in, clutching the broomstick that had once belonged to the Wicked Witch of the West, Oz the Terrible knew his gig was up. He could no more give the scarecrow some brains and the tin man a heart and the lion courage than he could flap his arms and fly back to his home in Omaha. Send Dorothy back to Kansas? Impossible. And he knew it.

HOLDING HANDS WITH THE WIZARD

Most of us know how the wizard felt. We hear our Savior telling us to tell the world about Him, and then we look around at the postmodern Oz and realize that we have nothing to say. That's how Coda felt. Although she was nearly eighty, she signed up for a one-day evangelism workshop led by her pastor. She sat with twenty other people during a Saturday morning and afternoon trying to finally overcome the fear that had kept her silent for far too long. Most of the workshop focused on using a small booklet to share the gospel.

"At least I don't have to memorize anything," Coda thought. "I can do that." She didn't like memorization, although working with her church's AWANA children made her realize she was better at memorizing than she had originally thought.

Coda's pastor went through each of the four sections of the booklet. She listened to his explanations beyond the words in the booklet. It all sounded so easy. She wondered why she always froze when the opportunity to witness presented itself. She came face-to-face with the answer immediately after the lunch break.

The group was going to divide into several pairs of partners to practice sharing the message of the booklets with each other. One person would play the role of a non-Christian, while the other tried to put into practice all the information discussed that morning. As people started pairing off, Coda's eyes raced around the room. She didn't want to be paired with John, who was too young and energetic for her to handle. The thought of trying to talk to him made this eighty-year-old nervous. Before the pastor could choose a partner for her, she slid over to Sally. The two were about the same age and had been friends for twenty years.

"I'll be the non-Christian," Coda volunteered. The pastor walked over to their corner of the room as Sally started her gospel presentation. Before she could get past the first page, Coda began firing off one question after another, asking everything from "where did Cain get his wife?" to "why does God allow suffering in the world?" By the time Coda hit her tenth question, Sally threw up her arms in despair.

"Why so many questions?" her pastor finally asked.

"This is what I always imagined would happen to me if I ever tried witnessing to someone," Coda confessed. "That's why I've never done it. I don't know what I would say." She looked at the floor, feeling guilty but also relieved to have the truth out in the open. For the first time she was honest with herself and God. She had not ignored the Great Commission out of a lack of compassion, but she hadn't shared her faith because the thought of engaging another person in a conversation about spiritual matters scared her to death.

HUMBUGS IN HIDING

The same scared feeling hits most of us in the pit of our stomachs when looking at the people of postmodern Oz. Tell these people about Jesus? To most, He's just another swear word. We don't know where we would start or how we could handle all the questions we'd surely be asked. And something deep inside of us is a little unsure about the whole idea of imposing our views on other people. Religion is such a private thing. Even bringing up the subject makes us nervous. Yet we can also hear echoing in our ears the words of Jesus in Acts 1:8: "You will be my witnesses" (NIV). The thought doesn't make most of us speak up; it usually just makes us feel guilty and defeated.

I know I'm painting with a broad brush by saying that most believers cower in fear at the thought of trying to engage postmodern culture with the gospel. Unfortunately, the broad brush fits. Statistics show that less than 10 percent of all believers actively share their faith. I see it in my home church. Every Sunday people are invited to tell the congregation stories of their friends who became Christians during the past seven days. The faces vary from time to time, but the same few people share on a regular basis. They don't really like the limelight. They're just involved in telling people about Christ. The rest of us sit there, slightly embarrassed, eager to move on to the next set of worship music.

WHY THE SILENCE?

Most of us followers of Jesus Christ do not actively share our faith with people around us for two reasons. First, we don't understand others and cannot speak their language. The problem affects every generation. Frances Schaeffer put it this way:

[The church's] responsibility is not only to hold to the basic, scriptural principles of the Christian faith, but to communicate these unchanging truths "into" the generation in which it is living. Every generation has the problem of learning how to speak meaningfully to its own age. It cannot be solved without an understanding of the changing existential situation which it faces. If we are to communicate the Christian faith effectively, we must know and understand the thought forms of our own generation.[1]

If we try to sell Jesus as a path to earthly happiness, we will soon be exposed as frauds.

The first section of this book addressed this problem of speaking different languages. We explored beneath the surface of things to try to understand how and why peo ple see the world the way they do. What we found is a land filled with people building lives without a center, people who accept every concept of truth as equally valid even when those concepts contradict each other. People wonder if anything is real, and most prefer false realities to the truth. People here communicate visually, through images and stories, rather than through a barrage of information. If we're to communicate our faith to the natives of this land, we must find ways to translate the message into their framework.

Which brings us to the second obstacle we face in trying to engage the people and culture surrounding us with the gospel. This is the one that sends us scurrying behind the curtain: We do not understand what we have to offer the people of Oz through the gospel. In spite of boldly proclaiming "Jesus is the answer," we aren't completely sure what we can translate into the language of the natives of this land. Outside of keeping a person out of hell, the urgency of having Christ in one's life escapes us. Sure, life goes better with Jesus, but that doesn't mean life will be more comfortable or easier. Personally, I've found the opposite to be the case. The more serious I am about walking with Christ the harder the road becomes. If we try to sell Jesus as a path to earthly happiness, we will soon be exposed as frauds. C.S. Lewis was once asked which of the religions of the world gives its followers the greatest happiness. He replied:

> *While it lasts, the religion of worshipping oneself is the best. I have an elderly acquaintance of about eighty, who has lived a life of unbroken selfishness and self-admiration from the earliest years, and is, more or less, I regret to say, one of the happiest men I know. From the moral point of view it is very difficult! I am not approaching the question from that angle. As you perhaps know, I haven't always been a Christian. I didn't go to religion to make me happy. I always knew a bottle of Port would do that.[2]*

Those of us who have walked with Jesus for any length of time know that Lewis is right, which brings us back to our dilemma. If not happiness and a more comfortable life, what do we have to offer the world?

We will explore the answer over the next several chapters. And here's what we will find: Postmodernism hasn't taken the Lord of the universe by surprise. It has not caused Him to wring His hands wondering what to do next. If God truly does control the flow of history (and the Bible makes it clear that He does) then this moment in history has occurred because He wants it to. He has placed you and me here because He wants us here as well. And He hasn't left us empty-handed.

Over the next few chapters, we will look at the essentials of the gospel and the foundations of the Christian faith. They intersect the culture of postmodern Oz at its point of greatest need. In a very real sense, the twenty-first century is like the first. Two thousand years ago God orchestrated the flow of history to prepare the environment in which the gospel would be spread. From the construction of the Roman roads, which made travel for Paul and his companions easier, to the widespread use of Greek, which tore down language barriers, Jesus launched the gospel in a time in which it caught ahold of people and spread like wildfire.

In these early days of the new millennium, the cultural landscape is very much the same. Some call this a post-Christian world, yet we could also call it pre-Christian. People have tried everything this world has to offer and found themselves still empty. Every substitute for God that the human race has looked to for hope and purpose has left them wanting. Now they long for something substantial, something to make them feel alive, something real. What we often moan as a tragedy is in fact a blessing from God. The depressing moments and inner emptiness can lead a person to the True God. Francis Schaeffer reached the following conclusion as he surveyed the cultural landscape that gave birth to postmodernism:

> We should be pleased that the romanticism of yesterday has been destroyed. In many ways this makes our task of presenting Christianity to modern man easier than it was for our forefathers . . . Already men are partway to the gospel, for they too believe that man is dead, *dead in the sense of being meaningless.*[3]

The postmodern world hungers for the very thing God offers through the gospel. And He dropped you and me in this place as His spokespeople. He didn't place us here to argue or start programs or deliver pre-packaged sales pitches. Instead, He left us in Oz to share the hope that the world is dying to hear.

CHAPTER EIGHT

X Faith

Let the dead bury the dead." He said it. Someone in the back probably thought that he was an insensitive jerk. How can one corpse bury another? He should have just come right out and told the guy to get lost. The dead burying the dead comment was just as subtle. When the man asked the question that brought this reply, he wasn't trying to be cute. "I'll follow you," he had said to the Teacher, "but first let me go and bury my father."

"Let the dead bury the dead" was all he heard in response. So he left. No sense staying where you aren't wanted.

The Teacher was like that. He offended people. To His critics He appeared to go out of His way to question conventional thinking. He was always breaking the rules and doing what people assumed He shouldn't be doing. And He never offered apologies to those who were insulted by His message. His closest friends asked Him one day,

"Don't you know you offended the religious leaders with what you said?"

"Leave them," He replied, "they are blind guides leading their followers into a pit." So much for diplomacy. So much for tact. If you didn't like what He had to say, you were cordially invited to leave.

And people did leave, by the droves. He told people to drop everything and follow Him. When a rich man expressed interest in becoming His follower, the Teacher told him to sell all his possessions and give them to the poor. That the rich man walked away rather than throw a garage sale for charity shouldn't surprise anyone. When another man asked for permission to go and say goodbye to his family, the Teacher basically told him that if he left he might as well not come back. "Anyone who loves his father or mother more than me is not worthy of me; anyone who loves his son or daughter more than me is not worthy of me; and anyone who does not take his cross and follow me is not worthy of me" (Matthew 10:37–38 NIV).

> Following Christ bears little resemblance to becoming an upstanding member of a comfortable community.

The man was a radical. He didn't spout pithy little clichés designed to make people feel better about themselves, and He didn't protect the status quo. He said, "I didn't come to bring peace, but conflict. I came to set a man against his family and a brother against a brother." Everyone who came in contact with Him faced a choice. They could accept His message and give up their lives to follow Him, or they could walk away. Radical. Revolutionary. Dangerous. His life, words, and demands of His disciples—they all pushed societal norms to the edge. He not only questioned authority, He claimed to *be* the ultimate Authority.

That's why they killed Him.

But He wouldn't stay dead. Three days after they put Him to death He walked out of the grave. A squad of armed guards fell down like dead men at the sight of Him. No one tried to shove Him back into His tomb or put a spear into Him to finish Him off for good. Instead they hit the dirt and hoped they would never see such a sight again. The story would sound like a scene from some low-budget thriller showing late at night on the Sci-Fi channel if it weren't true. The man walking out of the grave didn't look like a ghoul. The guards might have found some explanation for that. But what they saw scared them to death. Instead of a walking corpse, they saw glory that shone like the sun. They fell to the ground for they knew they weren't in the presence of a ghost, but a god, the Son of God who backed up His call for absolute commitment by rising from the dead.

And He is the one thing we have to offer people of Oz that they cannot live without. Our message to Oz centers on the Radical. We echo His words as we call people to leave everything behind to follow Him. Those who would follow Jesus don't just have to be willing to die for Him. They surrender their entire lives—their hopes, their dreams, their plans, their possessions, their talents, everything that makes them who they are—to the One who says, "Follow Me." Nothing about Him is safe or comfortable or respectable, nor does becoming His follower bear much resemblance to becoming an upstanding member of the community. Following the Radical is dangerous. And frightening. And unlike any of our preconceived ideas. The only word for it is X faith, extreme faith, faith that moves you from being a fan of Jesus or an aficionado of his teachings to being an all-out, nothing-held-back radical for Christ yourself. This is our message to Oz.

JESUS AND OZ

This radical Jesus may seem out-of-step with a twenty-first century audience. Not long ago I ventured into a New Age bookstore as part of a research project. The store itself was a one-hundred-year-old house with bookshelves around what used to be the parlor. Celtic instrumental music bounced off the wooden floors and filled the room. Books on angels and crystals and communicating with dead relatives were displayed in prominent places around the main room. A large pyramid made of copper tubing sat in an adjoining room, and in the center of the pyramid lay a baby in a portable crib.

The baby's mother came out of a room in the back, picked him up, and asked if I needed any help. "If I could, I would like to ask you a few questions, if you have time," I said.

No one else was in the store, and she gave a perky, "Sure, that would be great," in response. I started off with a few questions about how long she'd worked there and if this was just a job to her or if she used the products she sold. Since her baby had just been lying in the middle of a giant pyramid, I felt pretty confident of her answer.

She downplayed the magical power of the pyramid by saying, "It's the brightest place in the store. He likes playing there." She went on to talk about which of the books were her favorites and the changes in her life that had come from "getting in touch with the spiritual side." Our conversation shifted to her use of crystals and other good-luck charms, as well as her belief that the dead often give life-changing messages from beyond the grave.

"So what do you think about Jesus?" I asked.

She gave her child a warm hug, smiled and said, "Oh, we just love Jesus. Don't we, sweetheart?" She continued, "In fact, I've gone to church my whole life. I'm Presbyterian and never miss a Sunday." A little taken aback by her answer, I asked a few more questions. It soon became apparent that the Jesus she believed in was more of a symbol of unconditional love than a real Person who once walked on this earth.

This conception of the Son of God is very common in Oz. It can be heard on daytime talk shows and acceptance speeches at awards shows. Talk of Jesus is everywhere, but most people don't understand who He truly is.

HISTORICAL JESUS

Jesus was a subversive. Everything He said called into doubt the entire world system. The One who prior to His trip to earth sat on heaven's throne wasn't impressed with something as insignificant as wealth or fame or power. Not only did He refuse to give in to the world's temptations, He told His followers to turn their backs on everything that the world calls important. Throwing your lot in with Jesus put you on the outs with the rest of the world and set you apart as different. Not everyone who started the journey stuck with it. And Jesus never chased after those who drifted away. If anything, He upped the stakes in the presence of His followers who remained.

When a large group started to leave, He turned to the twelve disciples and, in essence, said, "What about you? There's the door. Leave if you want." Peter responded for the rest of the group with words that describe what it means to follow Jesus: "Lord, to whom would we go? You alone have the words that give eternal life" (John 6:68).

Where else would we go? Where else would we turn? No matter the cost, I must follow Him. From the beginning of time this has been the confession of those who follow God by faith. Abel, one of the first followers of God, paid for his devotion with his life. Abraham turned his back on his family, moved 2,000 miles, and lived in a tent the rest of his life, all because God said, "Come, follow Me." Moses rejected life as a prince over Egypt, choosing instead a lifetime of oppression in order that he might fully serve his Lord.

The stories go on and on. They fill the pages of both the Old and New Testament. Jesus was a radical, and following Him is a radical thing. It calls for a life of complete surrender and total commitment.

NO PLACE TO HIDE

And that's where most of us start getting very uncomfortable. Before I can call others to follow this Radical, I have to follow Him myself. The more I listen to His voice, the more I find myself hoping I can find some way to soften the blows of His commands. Maybe I'm the only one who finds himself thinking, "Surely that doesn't mean *me*," when I read Jesus saying something like, "If anyone comes to me and does not hate his father and mother, his wife and children, his brothers and sisters—yes, even his own life—he cannot be my disciple. And anyone who does not carry his cross and follow me cannot be my disciple" (Luke 14:26–27 NIV).

Jesus doesn't just mean I must love Him more than my father or mother or my wife or my children or even my own life. He is telling me my love for Him must be so overwhelmingly greater than my love for any of these others that, in comparison to my love for Him, I hate everyone else. Do I? Oh yeah, sure, no problem (with a wink, a wink and a sharp clearing of my throat). Don't you? I'm glad that voices don't crack in books.

When He walked up and down the roads of Judea, Jesus did more than ask people to invite Him into their lives. His appeals didn't have the same amount of polish as gospel tracts. "If anyone would come after me," He said, "he must deny himself and take up his cross and follow me. For whoever wants to save his life will lose it, but whoever loses his life for me will find it" (Matthew 16:24–25 NIV). His words rang in their ears as they stood at the foot of the cross watching Him die. "If I'm going to be His follower," John must have thought, "this is what I have to look forward to."

And this is the message we carry to Oz. We bring them Jesus, the Radical who demands that they follow Him with nothing held back. He isn't "Jesus the life problem-solver" or "the marriage-fixer-upper" or "the giver-of-sound-advice-for-raising-children." Nor is He "Jesus the make-me-feel-good-about-myself Savior." He is the Son of God. He is the Radical who died and rose again. And He calls for all people everywhere to deny themselves, take up their crosses, and follow Him. Even the people of Oz.

CHAPTER NINE

The Real World

Caleb stood from his desk with a groan. His back was stiff from sitting too long. He bent from side to side, trying to work out the kinks. "Caffeine," he said. "I need some caffeine." Since the only thing in his small refrigerator in the corner was a jar with three olives floating in yellow liquid, Caleb rummaged through his top desk drawer for change. He usually avoided the soda machine in the dorm basement since it only carried Coke products. Mello-Yello didn't deliver the kick of Mountain Dew, but it would do in a pinch. Caleb started toward his door and looked back at the stack of books piled around his computer keyboard. "Philosophy, I had to go and take philosophy," he huffed as he went off in search of his caffeine fix.

He took his time walking down the four flights of stairs from his third-floor room to the basement. The quicker he bought a can of soda, the quicker he had to go back to his room and face his philosophy paper. For the first few weeks of the semester, he'd enjoyed the class. The professor had introduced him to ways of seeing the world that he'd never thought about before. And this was done without telling the class what to think. Each time the professor had seemed to land on some position, he quickly did an about-face. "I love playing the devil's advocate," he'd said over and over. He had succeeded in making his students think.

As Caleb plodded down the stairs, he could do nothing but think. And right now all he could think of was how badly he didn't want to write this paper. "What a stupid question," he said to the stairway walls. "Why does anything exist rather than nothing? Like I know or care." He let out a long sigh and pushed the basement door open. The smell of laundry detergent and dryer sheets hit him in the face. "Why does anything exist," he thought. "Why? Who comes up with questions like these?" The soda machine was out of Mello-Yello. It was out of everything except Sprite Remix. "Great, the one drink that doesn't have caffeine. No thanks," he said and started back to his room. "Maybe I should learn to like coffee."

Rather than heading back upstairs, Caleb decided to go outside for some fresh air. Leaves crunched under his feet, and the cool, autumn nighttime air felt good after being confined in his stale dorm for most of the evening. A full moon lit the campus. "Why does anything exist?" he asked himself as he turned off the sidewalk and walked across the commons toward the dining hall. It wasn't open at this time of night, but he hoped he might find a soda machine that wasn't empty. He glanced up at the night sky and sighed. "Why does *anything* exist? Why do those stars exist?" Looking down at the ground passing under his feet, he thought, "Why does the grass exist? And why are there trees?"

The more he turned the question over and over in his mind, the more he realized that he'd asked the question before he received this assignment. He'd never phrased it quite this way, but it had been in his head. "Why does anything exist, and why do I exist? Why is there something rather than nothing?" He'd felt the question when his high school sophomore-year science teacher talked about how the universe sprang into existence with the Big Bang. And the question popped in his mind in the form of a dull wondering when he went to a friend's church and the youth leader talked about Adam and Eve. Everything he'd ever been taught about the origins of life always focused on the how, never the why. And now he could think of nothing else. Why does anything exist? As he turned back toward his dorm, he realized that he had no idea what the answer could possibly be. And he also knew he had to fill up five pages with something.[1]

TELL ME WHY

Caleb wrestled with the question that has troubled mankind since the beginning of time. Jean-Paul Sartre called it the first great philosophical question. Why does anything exist rather than nothing? The more science discovers about the nature of the universe, the louder the question grows. All of the laws of physics that govern this universe point to the fact that life had to spring forth. It could not be stopped. Novelist Michael Crichton put it this way through one of his characters in *Jurassic Park*, "Life breaks free. Life expands to new territories. Painfully, perhaps even dangerously. But life finds a way."[2]

Life finds a way because our universe is fine-tuned for life. There are plenty of examples and well-known scientific facts documented in several places. For instance, if the strong nuclear force that determines the rate at which our sun burns its fuel were changed by a mere 1 percent, the sun would explode in less than one second. But the laws of physics show that the sun and other stars burn their fuel slowly, giving them the potential to last billions of years.

Astronomers have also found that if the matter that "came out of the Big Bang" had emerged in a slightly different pattern, life could not exist anywhere in the universe. Yet the original matter moved in a precise way, which made sure life would not only exist, but thrive. And these are only the tip of the iceberg. Professor Martin Rees of the Institute of Astronomy in Cambridge said, "Wherever physicists look, they see examples of fine-tuning [for life]."[3]

WELCOME TO THE MULTIVERSE

The way in which all of the laws of physics work together to produce life leaves the postmodern world with an uncomfortable choice. The odds against life emerging by chance are small enough as to be impossible.[4] But that doesn't mean that people in Oz are ready to embrace the idea that God made everything. A new explanation for the universe's fine-tuning for life has emerged, which is becoming more and more accepted. The emerging postmodern view is that the inevitable existence of life in our universe is evidence of the existence of an infinite number of parallel universes, some of which support life, some of which do not.

I know it sounds like I've been watching too many

episodes of *Star Trek* where parallel universes have been a mainstay since Captain Kirk came face-to-face with his evil twin, yet the idea has come into the mainstream. It appeared in the August 2003 issue of *National Geographic Magazine* and was the central idea behind Michael Crichton's novel and the movie *Timeline*.

The theory of parallel universes, or a multiverse, simply states that our universe is just one of an infinite number of universes which continually split off at the quantum level. Professor Max Tegmark of the University of Pennsylvania calls this the ultimate ensemble, where every possible combination of the laws of physics is played out.[5] In one universe stars burn slowly, in another they burn up in an instant, in another they never formed at all. And new universes are being created all the time, splitting from one another to allow every possible action and reaction to come to pass.

> If absolute standards of right and wrong do not exist, then every law is nothing more than a statement of preference.

All these parallel universes sit side by side like bubbles in foam, occupying an infinite amount of space. Backers of the theory of the multiverse find evidence for their position in data sent back from the Wilkinson Microwave Anisotropy Probe satellite.[6]

NEXT QUESTION, PLEASE

The idea that life exists in our universe because life doesn't exist in other universes doesn't answer the question that sent Caleb off in search of caffeine. The theory doesn't say why life exists; it simply addresses *how* it came about. It can't answer the other question Caleb had thrust upon him after he arrived at college. A universe which occurred by chance, no matter how many of them there may be, cannot explain why some actions are right and some are wrong. Laws and rules are therefore nothing more than the end result of thousands of years of social evolution.

Caleb had already heard this idea, but he couldn't make it fit into the way he saw the world. If good and bad and right and wrong are human creations which shift and change with the times, then every act is morally neutral. Caleb's sociology professor had already sprung that one on him. She liked to say that even in a society of saints there would be sinners. Yet the more he listened, the more he asked how a morally neutral understanding of human actions could explain the difference between helping a little old lady across the street and shoving her in front of a bus. If absolute standards of right and wrong do not exist, then every law is nothing more than a statement of preference. Caleb wondered if his sociology professor would have such an enlightened view if he took it to its logical conclusion and cheated his way through her class. Somehow he doubted that she would.

THE REAL WORLD

These questions leave Caleb and all the residents of Oz in a very uncomfortable position. The way they see the world doesn't explain the real world that surrounds them. Deep down they long for something real—they long for meaning and purpose in life. Yet their worldview tells them that there is no meaning. There is no purpose. Life just is. Deal with it. But no one wants to deal with it. To admit there is no meaning behind the existence of life is to admit that I am little more than a cosmic accident. Life has no meaning. No purpose. No point. No hope. Yet everything within the human species cries out that life has to matter. There has to be a purpose for our lives.

And that's what we have to offer to Caleb and other residents of Oz. The Bible describes the physical realm as a unique creation, which flowed out of the infinite artistry of God. Cosmic accidents, even on a grand scale, don't produce beauty by chance, yet beauty and wonder fill every corner of the universe. From nebulas in obscure corners of the galaxy exploding with color that only God enjoyed until the Hubble telescope started orbiting the earth, to wildflowers blooming alongside a Texas highway, the universe leaves us in awe at the artistic eye of its Creator.

And this universe has a purpose. The psalmist said it best, "The heavens tell of the glory of God. The skies display his marvelous craftsmanship" (Psalm 19:1). They declare God's glory for that is why they exist. Revelation 4:11 says, "For [God] created everything, and it is for [His] pleasure that they exist and were created." The universe exists to bring glory to God. That's why it is. And the universe does a wonderful job of it (*not* including the human race).

Our wars, bombs, lies, and abuse of one another are examples of how we stand out as a broken part of creation. Something is wrong with us, and we know it. Yet at the same time, the human race shows artistry and creativity that cannot be explained away. We're different from the rest of animals on this planet no matter how many times we call the chimps down at the zoo our distant cousins. Chimps don't take a pile of Popsicle sticks and build bridges with them. People do. We create with anything and everything. And we ask questions and seek answers to the mysteries of the universe. Thousands of years of frustration can't stop us from asking. We're different. We're more than mere animals. And the people of Oz know it. They just don't know how or why.

TRUE REALITY

The story of the Bible gives us the answer. It gives real insight into why we are what we are. The Bible tells us we were created in the image of God. That's why we draw and paint and write and build and turn the act of providing fuel for the body into an art form. But the story doesn't stop there. People are cruel to one another and do wrong with the greatest of ease because of a simple three-letter word that no one wants to acknowledge anymore: sin. The human race is fallen and flawed because it chose to disobey God. Every person who draws a breath does wrong by nature and by choice because he is a sinner. Stephen King said it well in his book *The Stand:* "Man may have been made in the image of God, but human society was made in the image of His opposite number, and is always trying to get back home."[7]

These two aspects of reality can best be seen through the Cross of Jesus Christ. There we see God's purpose for creation and the problem of sin collide once and for all. Jesus Christ, through whom all things were created (John 1; Colossians 1:15–17), died at the hands of His creation made in His image. Jesus died for a reason, to restore fallen human beings to God and to His original purpose for making them. This isn't just some story or fuel for an argument with an atheist. The Cross reveals the real world to a land that doesn't believe reality exists. The question on the lips of the people in Oz is not what is true, but what is real. The Cross is real. And through the Cross, the universe and the people who inhabit it become real as well.

CHAPTER TEN

A Reason
for Being

Brian didn't ask a question, but Chaplain Bob gave him an answer anyway. Questions were far from Brian's mind. He wanted to share some exciting news with the chaplain, news that he had accepted Jesus as his Savior. It was a big step for a thirteen-year-old boy living in a juvenile detention center outside of Dallas, Texas. Some people think boys in Brian's shoes turn to God out of desperation after finding themselves in a scary situation. That may be true, but don't many people turn to God when life becomes frightening? God had Brian's full and undivided attention, and Brian responded by saying yes to Jesus.

And that's why he walked into Chaplain Bob's office that Tuesday afternoon. Brian wanted to tell the man who kept talking about Jesus what he had finally decided. He did not exude emotion nor did his voice explode with enthusiasm. When he made it into the chaplain's office, Brian appeared to be a little nervous. He seemed unsure about what he was supposed to say. Hearing the words "I've decided to follow Jesus" come out of his mouth for the first time seemed to surprise him. I'm not sure if what happened next surprised Brian, but it surprised me when I saw it.

Chaplain Bob was sitting at his desk looking over a piece of paper when Brian walked through the door. Brian cleared his throat to get Bob's attention and told him why he was there. A smile broke out across Chaplain Bob's face. "That's great," he said, "that's just great." The chaplain reached into his desk, pulled out a book called *A Survival Kit for New Believers,* and handed it to Brian. "Now you take this and read it," the chaplain said. "It will tell you a lot of what you need to know about what it means to follow Jesus." Brian took the book and began thumbing through it. He looked up as Chaplain Bob continued, "And you need to know, you are a Christian now, and that means you don't cuss, you don't smoke, you don't chew tobacco, you don't drink, you don't chase women, and you don't go to rock 'n' roll concerts. Do you understand?"

Brian nodded his head to say yes, but his excitement had evaporated. He stopped thumbing through the *Survival Kit,* lowered his eyes, and walked out of the chaplain's office. My mouth dropped. After he was gone, Chaplain Bob turned to me and said, "You just have to make it clear what you expect out of these boys. You have to make it clear what God wants out of them as well. Some of 'em, they turn to Jesus just because they got themselves in trouble. Our job is to make sure we keep 'em on the right road." I didn't argue the point since I was a first year Bible-college student applying for an assistant chaplain's position, but I did withdraw my application.

HAVEN'T I HEARD THIS BEFORE?

People who do not know Jesus Christ personally may not have heard Chaplain Bob's speech, but they feel like they know it by heart. In the eyes of most, Christianity is a religion of don'ts. Don't drink. Don't dance. Don't cuss. Don't smoke. Above all, don't enjoy life. Most people have probably never been told this is what it means to be a Christian. They simply assumed this is what it had to mean since the vocal believers they knew in high school or college didn't drink or cuss or smoke or sleep around or do any of the things that those outside the faith believe constitute a good time. Those who do not have a dynamic relationship with Christ cannot understand why anyone wouldn't do what they love to do.

And therein lies one of the greatest barriers we face as we try to reach out to residents of a postmodern Oz. Those we're trying to reach reject our message without even hearing it. But if they did take the time to listen, they would find that the gospel offers three things that this world can never give: value, purpose, and freedom. In short, a relationship with Christ would provide them with an identity and sense of worth that they've never known before. Without this they are stuck in a vicious cycle, which slowly but surely strips them of their value.

Life in the postmodern multiverse is very dehumanizing and devaluing. From the earliest moments of life, people here are told that they are little more than the final product of time plus chance. Life isn't a miracle and neither are we. We're nothing more than animals—advanced animals, but animals nonetheless. Sure, we have rights, but our rights shouldn't trample on the rights of the billions of other species that inhabit this fragile planet. A human being is no more special and no more worthy of rights and privileges than a dog or a cow or a slug. After all, we're all just carbon-based life-forms in the process of evolving into other carbon-based life-forms.

But that isn't the end of the depressing news. The scientific world continues to say that the universe is a machine and human beings are just cogs in that machine. People do the things they do, not out of choice, but because this is what they are pre-programmed to do. Our genetic code, our environment, our education, and our family background all work together to make us who we are. Rather than being free to do whatever we want, we simply do what nature and environmental forces cause us to do. At the same time we're told to think good thoughts about ourselves because a strong self-image produces healthier, happier, more productive citizens. This leads to a kind of schizophrenia, where on the one hand we are little more than animals whose behavior is predetermined by instinct and hundreds of thousands of years of evolution, and on the other we're supposed to be happy because we're somebody special.

VALUE

Into this very strange mix of conflicting ideas steps the God who created the heavens and earth. Many people look away because they think that in His hands is an etched-in-stone list of things they should not do. They are partially correct. The Bible does contain many laws that begin with "Thou shalt not . . ." Yet His commands are only part of the story. The heart of the law, and the heart of the Christian message, was summed up by Moses:

And now, Israel, what does the LORD your God require of you? He requires you to fear him, to live according to his will, to love and worship him with all your heart and soul, and to obey the LORD's commands and laws that I am giving you today for your own good. The highest heavens and the earth and everything in it all belong to the LORD your God. Yet the LORD chose your ancestors as the objects of his love. *(Deuteronomy 10:12-15)*

God's message to the human race is this: I love you and want to enter into a relationship with you. This relationship cannot be won or maintained by keeping a list of dos and don'ts. As Francis Schaeffer said:

The true Christian life, true spirituality, is not merely a negative not-doing of any small list of things. Even if the list began as a very excellent list of things to beware of in that particular historic setting, we must still emphasize that the Christian life, or true spirituality, is more than refraining from a certain external list of taboos in a mechanical way.[1]

Through us believers, God's spokespeople on earth, Christ offers our neighbors much more than a list of things not to do. He offers them life, the kind of life Jesus said that He came to give in all its fullness (John 10:10). The life He brings gives human beings true value. In the last chapter, we touched on the fact that God made people in His image. Because of this, individuals matter. Every person, no matter how small or poor or invisible, has value in the eyes of God because He made them to be like Himself.

But the message of the Bible doesn't stop there. One of the simplest Bible verses is also the most profound, "For

God so loved the world that he gave his only Son, so that everyone who believes in him will not perish but have eternal life" (John 3:16). Every person has intrinsic value in the eyes of God. That's the message we carry to Oz. You are more than an animal. You are more than a cog in the cosmic machine. You are a human being, dearly loved by God, and one who matters in His eyes.

PURPOSE

God values human beings, and He has a purpose for each and every one of us. People in Oz aren't looking for *the* meaning of life. They stopped searching for a big-picture answer that will bring all of the complexities of life together in one handy, easy-to-understand, and easy-to-believe system. But they do long to find meaning and purpose *in* life. They want to make a difference and matter in this world. A Yankelovich survey asked what question people would ask God if they knew they would get an immediate and direct answer. The results showed that 34 percent would ask, "What's my purpose here?"[2]

> We come with the good news of how life can matter now and forever.

And God gives a very simple answer, an answer so basic most people stumble over it. Rick Warren put it this way in his best-seller, *The Purpose Driven Life*: "You were made by God and for God—until you understand that, life will never make sense."[3]

This is the message we carry to Oz. You matter. You have value. And God has a purpose for your life. The "don't cuss, don't smoke, don't chew tobacco, don't drink, don't chase women, and don't go to rock 'n' roll concerts" approach to the Christian life misses God's point. God said through the apostle Paul, "For we are God's masterpiece. He has created us anew in Christ Jesus, so that we can do the good things he planned for us long ago" (Ephesians 2:10). As we walk down the yellow brick road into the Emerald City, we carry more than information about how people can escape hell and gain entrance into heaven. We come with the good news of how life can matter now and forever. Through Christ we can do more than make a difference by planting a few trees and flowers to make neighborhoods look nice. In Him, the work we do counts for eternity as we fulfill His eternal purpose for our lives. The world is asking, "What on earth am I here for?" As missionaries to Oz, we have the answer.

FREEDOM

Lists can never capture the essence of the good news that we bring to Oz because lists have a way of ensnaring us. Even lists of good things grab us and hold us down. Jesus didn't die to chain us to a list. He came to set us free. "It is for freedom that Christ has set us free," Galatians 5:1 (NIV) declares. This is freedom to embrace our identity and value as a part of God's family. Outside of Him we are slaves to sin, held captive by Satan to do his evil will (2 Timothy 2:26). But Jesus breaks the chains of sin and sets us free to love and serve Him. Within our freedom in Christ is the liberty to fully express the image of God in us through every means possible.

So many people who have not yet experienced freedom in Christ assume that Christianity throws a chain around your neck. Christians have to go to church. They have to abstain from alcohol. They have to watch nothing but G-rated films and wholesome family shows like the ones starring Steve Urkel. Again, this misses the point. The freedom we have in Christ begins with the freedom to enter His presence whenever we desire. He gives us freedom from sin, from guilt, from the constant condemnation we lived under before finding Him. And this freedom allows me to be fully a creature made in the image of God, glorifying Him with everything I do.

This is what we have to offer Oz. Value. Purpose. Freedom. Our message is a message of life, not a list of dos and don'ts. Perhaps the reason so many people find this hard to believe is they see so little of it in the lives of the people they know who profess to be followers of Jesus.

Part Three
Wizard or Humbug?

Oz, left to himself, smiled to think of his success in giving the Scarecrow and the Tin Woodman and the Lion exactly what they thought they wanted. "How can I help being a humbug," he said, "when all these people make me do things that everybody knows can't be done? It was easy to make the Scarecrow and the Lion and the Woodman happy, because they imagined I could do anything. But it will take more than imagination to carry Dorothy back to Kansas, and I'm sure I don't know how it can be done."

CHAPTER ELEVEN

Do Something

I could hear my heartbeat pounding in my ears. "Calm down," I told myself over and over, to no avail. My adrenal glands had already hit overdrive, and the rest of my body was racing to catch up. The mask over my face distorted my vision, and the self-contained breathing apparatus couldn't keep up with my demand for oxygen. I knew that if I didn't settle down, the self-contained breathing apparatus on my back would soon run out of air, and I would have to back out of the smoke-filled building. Another thought snapped into my head, which prevented me from regaining my composure: I had no idea what I was doing.

Before the alarm went off, I thought I knew exactly what I would do in this situation. Months of training had made parts of my job as a firefighter automatic. I could don an air pack quicker than I could throw on a shirt. Hoses and nozzles had become second nature. In my mind I had rehearsed what to do at a fire scene, from connecting the hose to the hydrant to crawling through a smoky room in search of fire and survivors. Along the way I'd also become pretty good at cleaning bathrooms and fire-station floors and all the other menial tasks rookie firefighters have to do. I thought I had a handle on my chosen profession.

And then I found myself crawling through a second floor window of a three-story fraternity house. Smoke poured out of all the windows while a snorkel truck dumped water through the roof. Hoses snaked across the parking lot and lawn and split off in several directions at the doorways. Firefighters from three or four stations darted in and out of the building. One of the senior firefighters from my station, a guy we called Hack, grabbed me and told me to follow him.

Making disciples in the postmodern world cannot be reduced to a program.

As we climbed the ladder and crawled through the window, my heartbeat kept getting faster and faster. I sucked in gulps of air. This was the moment I had been waiting for, and I found myself blowing it. My mind went blank. "What am I supposed to do?" I screamed at myself in my mind and started to freeze. Hack turned and looked at me. "Do something," he yelled, "even if it's wrong!"

That was our philosophy on the C-crew at station three. Don't just stand there. Do something. Whatever we did would probably help, since it was unlikely any firefighter, no matter how inexperienced, would throw kerosene instead of water on a burning building. When you have an idea of what you need to do, you do it. The fire isn't going to put itself out.

All the talk about a mission to Oz eventually comes down to the same decision. We have to do something. Left to itself, the culture will continue to spiral downward. People who don't know Christ aren't going to find Him on their own. We must do something, and at this stage we should have a pretty good handle on what needs to be done. We've surveyed the landscape of Oz and understand the common ways of thinking. And we've explored the ways God's truth intersects the lives of postmodern people at their point of greatest need. There's only one thing left to do. It's time to do something.

But what?

The answer hasn't changed in 2,000 years. Firefighters fight fire. Followers of Jesus Christ make more disciples of Christ. Jesus, Himself, laid out the unchanging mission of every believer: "Go and make disciples of all the nations, baptizing them in the name of the Father and the Son and the Holy Spirit. Teach these new disciples to obey all the commands I have given you. And be sure of this: I am with you always, even to the end of the age" (Matthew 28:19–20).

The last few chapters will explore how we can carry out this mandate in our own generation. Before we jump in, we need to understand one truth. Making disciples in the postmodern world cannot be reduced to a program. There is no one-size-fits-all approach, no simple three-, four-, or forty-step formula to memorize and repeat by rote. That doesn't work here. We need to heed the words of Francis Schaeffer:

As we turn to consider in more detail how we may speak to people of the twentieth century, we must emphasize first of all that we cannot apply mechanical rules . . . Each person must be dealt with as an individual, not as a case or statistic or machine. If we would work with these people, we cannot apply the things we have dealt with in this book mechanically. We must look to the Lord in prayer, and to the work of the Holy Spirit, for the effective use of these things.[1]

The steps we will explore in the next few chapters are not an exhaustive treatment of everything anyone needs to know to make a difference in Oz. Nor are they especially profound or unique. Most will seem very basic. But that's always the place we need to begin. In spite of the unique characteristics of postmodern culture, some of the basic needs of human beings never change. What does change is the way in which these needs manifest themselves, and the methods by which they can be met.

Fighting fires and making disciples in the postmodern world are a lot alike. Neither will happen by accident. Nor is there a long line of volunteers waiting for the chance to be a part of the action. Both tasks are dirty, tiresome, difficult jobs that demand more than we can imagine. Yet in the end, the results are more than worth the effort.

CHAPTER TWELVE

More
than Words

Carl and I have the same conversation over and over. We may go six months without bringing the subject up, which will be followed by several days of intense e-mails flying back and forth. We're brutally honest with each other. That's what allows us to revisit the one subject that divides us. Carl doesn't believe in God. He dismisses the whole idea of religion as little more than a myth, and the notion of an all-powerful, good God as fairy-tale material. And I try to convince him otherwise.

I'm not the only Christian who talks to Carl about God, but he doesn't listen to most of them. The problem isn't the subject matter. No, something else keeps him from carrying on serious conversations about God with the well-meaning people who come into his office to try and save his soul. "I know a lot of people who go to church," Carl says, "but I know very few that I actually consider to be Christians. Most people I know who wear that label use God for their own selfish purposes." He paused, then added, "I think that really hurts the whole movement."

In Oz it doesn't just hurt the movement—it cripples it. Trying to reach people who reject the notion of experts and whose eyes glaze over when facts and figures start flying around the room is more than a problem of trying to find the right methodology or formula. Francis of Assisi's words to, "Preach the gospel at all times. When necessary use words," apply more now than ever before. Talk of God is cheap. The primary method by which we can fulfill our mission and make Christ known to a postmodern world is by becoming painfully authentic. We have to be real before our words will mean a thing. Even then the message of our life must be much louder than the words coming out of our mouths.

But what does it mean to be real?

REALITY 101

At its most basic level, being real means living a moral life. I hesitate to include this because it seems so obvious. The language a believer uses should be different, as should his sexual practices. Again, I almost feel silly including something so basic. This is like Religion 101, a step even nonbelievers can take. My friend Carl is one of the most moral people I know, and he questions the existence of God. If he can stay faithful to his wife and treat his customers with honesty and respect, how much more so should those of us who claim to have devoted our lives to Jesus Christ do the same?

Even still, this is the very place so many of us fail. It's not that we go out and commit one of the BIG sins, like murder or robbing a bank. Instead we find ourselves compromising on little things, shading the truth here and there when it proves profitable to do so. The acts don't have to be intentional to discredit our witness. All we have to do is share the worldview of unbelievers. "As long as American Christians model a faith based on complacency, convenience, and narcissism, living no differently from anyone else," George Barna says, "our evangelistic witness will be hollow."[1]

MORE THAN MORALITY

Living a moral life is the first step toward authenticity, but it barely scratches the surface. The one thing that truly sets followers of Jesus Christ apart is the relationship that they enjoy with Him. To be a Christian means loving the Lord more than anything else in the world. Both Moses and Jesus tell us to "love the Lord your God with all your heart, all your soul, all your mind, and all your strength" (Mark 12:30; Deuteronomy 6:5).

Being real means taking these words seriously and putting them into practice. Paul did. He found himself so in awe of God's love that he called everything else that this world had to offer nothing but garbage (Philippians 3:8). Christ's love controlled him and compelled him to share that love with others (2 Corinthians 5:14). By reading Paul's letters you realize that he never got over the wonder that God would love someone like him. He loved his Lord more than wealth or fame or even his own life. Nothing compared to Jesus, and he ached to be with Him. You can't fake this kind of passion for God. It is the mark of an authentic Christian.

BY THE BOOK

A passion for God will also translate into a passion for His Word. The two go hand in hand for we cannot know or love God without the Bible. And Romans 10:17 says, "Faith comes from listening to this message of good news—the Good News about Christ." His Word is the story of His goodness.

Israel's King David loved God's Word and praised Him saying, "Oh, how I love your law! I think about it all day long" (Psalm 119:97). The righteous, David said in Psalm 1, delight themselves in God's law and meditate on it day and night. True believers will share David's passion. God's Word ought not be something we peruse now and then at our leisure.

> Becoming real in Christ means becoming who He created me to be.

"People need more than bread for their life," Jesus said, "they must feed on every word of God" (Matthew 4:4). Unfortunately, fewer and fewer people who profess to believe in Jesus read the Bible in more than bits and pieces. Leonard Sweet calls this the crisis of evangelism in a postmodern world where Bible-believing churches are filled with people who don't read the Bible.[2] This isn't just a problem of young adults not knowing where to find the book of Nehemiah. As biblical illiteracy grows, people who claim to be born-again believers become more and more indistinguishable from the world in the way they think and act.

"Sixty-eight percent of evangelicals believe there is no such thing as moral truth," Charles Colson told me. "Pastors get up and say, 'The truth shall set you free,' meaning that Jesus will set a person free from sin and death. But people sitting in the pews often hear, 'My preference gives me the freedom to do anything I want.' That's a totally different idea."[3]

Becoming real in Christ means allowing the Bible to completely transform the way I understand the world around me and interact with it. We live in a culture that doubts everything. Reality doesn't exist in the eyes of many. Few people believe in moral truth, and fewer still believe in any absolutes beyond public opinion. If we are ever going to impact Oz, we must be different. God's truth as revealed through His Word must completely permeate our hearts and minds. "We must see God's truth as something that encompasses all of life," Colson said.[4] And we must see all of life through the lens of Scripture. Having this kind of biblical worldview goes beyond being able to quote verses in conversations with other people. It demands we read and believe and obey all of Scripture, from beginning to end. In the process God will change us completely. We will be transformed as our minds are renewed through the Word of life. Without this we are completely ill equipped to go into Oz to make disciples.

TURNING UP THE VOLUME

Our actions must demonstrate authentic Christianity to reach Oz, and so must our words. We need to carry on genuine conversations with the people we hope to reach. And this is the very point where this whole business of being a missionary to Oz gets hard. Honest, authentic conversations about God and Christ are difficult, messy, and risky. That's why every evangelism course I've ever taken or taught as a pastor focused on memorizing a canned approach that participants regurgitated to unbelievers. Many courses have told potential witnesses how to avoid a give-and-take conversation in order to keep the gospel presentation on track. If the person being witnessed to ever happened to interrupt at some point with a question, the witness was supposed to say, "That's a very good question. I'm glad you asked. And I'll get to it in just a moment, but first . . ." and then jump right back into the memorized presentation.

The canned approach implies that we have something to fear from an honest interchange of ideas. Perhaps we are afraid of being proven wrong or of being hit with a question we cannot answer. Yet if the gospel is true, it has nothing to fear from conversations with those who don't believe it. "It is prepared to face the consequences of being proved false," Schaeffer said, "and to say with Paul: If you find the body of Christ, the discussion is finished; let us eat and drink, for tomorrow we die."[5]

"I've heard plenty of canned sales pitches for God," Carl told me. "The people may not have meant them that way, but that's how they came across. They tried so hard to get all this information out about God and have me switch sides that they didn't have time for a real conversation. I don't mind talking about God. I even think about this stuff from time to time, but I don't want to listen to someone trying to shove God down my throat."

Most people in Oz echo Carl's sentiments. People today are more open to talking about spiritual matters than any time I can remember, but no one wants to listen to a lecture from a "God expert." For postmodern people, the experts might as well all be dead. People want to discover things for themselves. And they also have ideas about who God is and how He works. Their ideas may be completely wrong, but if we dismiss them all out of hand, they will dismiss our ideas without listening as well. In the same way, if our interest in the other person seems false, and we convey the idea that we only want to recruit them to our cause, the conversation won't last long.

What is needed are honest and open conversations centered on God. That's the only way we will gain a hearing in Oz. Yet we sometimes feel as though we have to present an ideal picture of the Christian life or no one will be interested in it. We think that if we talk about the struggles or the doubts or the days when it feels as though God is a million miles away and this whole Christianity thing isn't what it's cracked up to be that no one will listen. Therefore, we resort to clichés or we try to make it sound as though our life has been nothing but great since we accepted Christ as our Savior.

It's this sort of "God as the panacea for everything" that adds fuel to the skeptics' fire. They can see through our happy façade, as well they should. In the book of Job we see a collision between the life-is-wonderful-for-those-who-believe crowd and the raw, gritty, aching faith of Job. No one on earth compares to Job in terms of performance for God, yet he loses everything in one horrific day. His comforters are shocked when Job voices what anyone going through such a nightmare feels. They tried to pretend God would never allow His children to face such heartache. He always blesses the righteous, they maintained. Yet in the end, God rebuked the comforters and commended Job.

We need to show the same kind of honesty in our conversations with people in Oz. No clichés. No pretending faith fixes every problem. We need to convey a realistic picture of who God is and what He does in this world.

The Bible's message is realistic. We should be also as we try to convey its message to the postmodern world.

This is where being real in our Christian lives comes together with honesty in our conversations with non-Christians. We must be fully authentic in our walk with Christ, which means overflowing with love for Him and seeing the world through a consistent biblical world-view. Knowing His love and truth will then spill over into the conversations we have with people in Oz. Until the Bible transforms the way I understand the world around me and interact with its people, I don't have anything of substance to say. And unless I live out this new understanding of the world in my day-to-day life, no one will listen anyway.

CHAPTER THIRTEEN

Face-
to-Face

A chill crawled up Richard's back. He looked over at
Chuck, his prayer partner, and the sweat on Chuck's fore-
head told Richard that his friend felt it too. When their
team leader asked for volunteers, the task didn't seem so
scary. After all, they'd spent the better part of the past two
days walking around unsupervised on the yard of the
medium security prison in Chino, California. Richard and
Chuck had the run of the place, along with the other seventy-
five members of their prison ministry team. They ate with
inmates, spent time talking with them in their cells, and
took the never-ending stroll on the track around the
perimeter of the yard with one man after another.

Although the prison increased its usual contingent of
guards to take care of their guests, Richard knew that any
one of the prisoners who wanted to do them harm could
with the greatest of ease. But he wasn't at all worried.
When the sun began to sink over the western wall,

Richard felt a strong sense of satisfaction. He knew God had used him to make a difference in the lives of a few men, a difference that would last forever.

Yet as Richard waited with Chuck in the corridor outside of the HIV ward of the prison, that good feeling was long gone. HIV and AIDS were still both relatively unknown diseases on this evening in 1989. Richard had heard all the assurances that the disease could not be spread through casual contact, but knowing he was about to be locked into a room with fifty men with the disease made doubts creep into his head. His friend didn't help. "Nervous?" Chuck asked.

"Nah, piece of cake," Richard laughed as he answered.

"Yeah, you're probably right," Chuck answered, "but I wouldn't shake too many hands, not with that cut on your index finger." Chuck smiled as though he was trying to be funny. Richard looked down at his hand. He wasn't laughing.

Before Richard could think of anything to say in response, the gate opened. "Come on in, gentlemen," a guard smiled and said. "Make yourselves at home." The prison ministry volunteers entered the dayroom. Once they were all inside, a heavy steel door in the back of the room swung open and the permanent residents filed in. The prison ministry team lined up across the room, shaking hands with one man after another, telling them that they were glad to see them and asking where they were from. Most of the inmates gave nervous smiles in response along with one or two word answers as they made their way to tables and sat down.

Richard and Chuck stood with the other volunteers, shaking hands, making small talk. After most of the men were in the room, they started to walk over to a table on the far left-hand side to sit down with four inmates. But before they could take another step, Richard felt himself stop dead in his tracks. In reality, he did little more than pause for a moment or two, but to Richard, it felt like he stood there for five minutes. He couldn't believe his eyes. "I didn't know they kept women in this ward," were his first thoughts as he watched this inmate swish across the room. But this was no woman in spite of his long hair and makeup and polished nails. Richard didn't mean to stare, but this person's appearance left him more than a little shocked. Try as he might, he couldn't keep his jaw from dropping, nor could he completely suppress the laugh welling up from deep inside himself. Looking over at his friend, Richard saw Chuck had the exact same reaction. Regaining his composure, Richard finally walked on and sat down with a couple of more normal-looking inmates.

Richard and Chuck weren't alone. All the other volunteers steered clear of the most effeminate man most had ever seen. All that is except one prison ministry team member, a man named Thomas. Thomas walked straight over to the cross-dresser, stuck out his hand, and introduced himself. As he sat down, he didn't look the inmate over as if to say, "What's the matter with you?" Instead he treated the man with dignity and respect. For the next forty minutes or so, Thomas talked with the man who was shunned by many, listening to what he had to say. He didn't scold the man for his lifestyle that had caused him to be locked up and given him a disease that would one day take his life. Instead Thomas let God love this man through him.

This is the best picture I can find of what we are called to do as missionaries to Oz. Our mission is to invade postmodern culture with the love of God. But this isn't some syrupy, sentimental, fake-smile kind of love that never goes beyond polite talk or occasional kind deeds. The love that God wants to reveal to the postmodern world through us is real. It sits down with an outcast and says, "The One who spoke all of creation into existence desires a relationship with you."

THE HEART OF THE MISSION

And that's what makes this mission so difficult. Oz is filled with people who aren't very easy to love. They leave us doing what futurist Leonard Sweet calls the cultural cringe, "a hip rain-dance of hand-wringing, tongue-whanging, nose-whining, hot-water-bottle-clutching, pill-popping, teeth-gnashing to the tune of wailings and railings against the evils of the postmodern world (if not the flesh and the devil)."[1] We don't mean to cringe any more than Richard meant to have his skin crawl at the sight of the cross-dressing AIDS patient, but we can't help ourselves. So much about the postmodern world offends us, from the body piercings to the tattoos to the clothing styles to the immorality that parades across our television screens. Oz doesn't exactly endear itself to visitors.

Reaching Oz is more than a matter of understanding the fine points of postmodernism or learning to communicate in the thought forms of people today. The heart of our mission is loving people with more than words. Putting the love of Christ into action is "an attempt to move over and sit in the other person's place and see how his problems look to him."[2] It looks at people as individuals, not projects, recognizing their great value as bearers of the image of God.

Because human beings are created in God's image, every member of the human race craves love and kindness that can only be satisfied through meaningful relationships. Some writers call the desire for relationships and community a key characteristic of the postmodern generation, but the same could be said of every generation since fig leaves were the hottest thing in fashion. Blaise Pascal once said each human being has a God-shaped vacuum within his heart. We could also say each of us has another vacuum within our hearts, a vacuum that can only be filled with love from other human beings. God, Himself, said, "It is not good for the man to be alone" (Genesis 2:18). He also told us that our love for Him could best be shown by loving other people (1 John 4:20).

As followers of Christ and missionaries to the postmodern world, God has given us two ways to best show His love to others, both of which must be used for our mission to be effective. We must share His love as individuals and we must share His love as a community. You and I may never find ourselves face-to-face with a transvestite AIDS patient in the HIV ward of a prison, yet every day God brings unlovable people across our paths. If we listen closely we can hear Him whisper, "Let me love him through you." The ways in which He wants to demonstrate that love are only limited by our imagination and our willingness to yield to the Holy Spirit. He wants to use our actions, but He also enjoys using our reactions to disarm the skeptic and open a heart to His Son. Staying in tune with God (and out of tune with our natural, selfish instincts) takes a great deal of work and prayer. It takes us right back to the subject of the last chapter. Authentic Christians love others just as God loved them.

IT TAKES A COMMUNITY
TO MAKE A DISCIPLE

You and I can't fulfill our mission as followers of Christ by ourselves, especially the calling to be conveyors of God's love for the world. We need other people. We need to be surrounded by those who share our passion for Christ and the desire to make a difference in Oz. We need the community of believers, also known as the church.

The postmodern world has reawakened people to the absolute importance of community. Hillary Clinton tapped into this felt need when she wrote *It Takes a Village to Raise a Child.* Even her critics agreed with her central idea: Community matters and shapes our lives. Community and relationships have always been a part of the lives of believers through local churches, yet we live in a time when they are more important than ever. Stanley Grenz, author of *Beyond Foundationalism: Shaping Theology in a Postmodern Context,* calls community building the ultimate key to reaching people. In an interview with the postmodern ministry magazine *Next Wave,* Grenz went on to say, "The best apologetic we have in the postmodern context is the vibrant, local community of disciples who are loyal to Christ, that is, a community in which the power of the Spirit is transforming relationships. As many of my friends in Intervarsity Christian Fellowship tell me, postmodern persons are converted to the community before they are converted to Christ."[3]

The idea is so simple it almost seems radical. One of the best ways to reach people in the postmodern world is to build communities of believers who genuinely love other people and welcome them into the family with open arms. It worked for Dan. Dan never cared much about church. When pressed, he would say he was a Christian. He even had the baptismal certificate somewhere in his parents' attic to prove it, but deep down he knew better. Most Christians he knew never made a living hustling pool. Dan did. More than once he watched a man walk away from the pool table, face ashen, shoulders slumped, as Dan held the man's payroll check in his hand. If he stopped to digest the scene unfolding before him, feelings of guilt would sweep over him. So Dan didn't think about it. He chose not to care.

The biggest factors, which kept him coming back and softened his heart to the gospel, were the relationships he was welcomed into by the church community.

Most Christians Dan knew never came within a heartbeat of killing another human being. He had. To this day Dan doesn't know what stopped him from pulling the trigger on the .44 Magnum he pressed into the temple of the man he caught in bed with his wife. He wanted to kill this man, but something stopped him. Instead Dan beat the man senseless, leaving him bleeding on the floor. The first policeman on the scene saved two lives. Instead of taking Dan to jail, he took him to a mental health facility. As it turns out, the policeman had caught his own wife in an act of infidelity just a few months earlier. He knew how Dan felt and wanted to help him rather than lock him up.

Since then, Dan turned his life around and found respectability. He stopped hustling pool and abandoned the seamy side of town. A few years after nearly forfeiting his freedom forever, he met a Christian woman who didn't care about his past. The two were married three years later and built a comfortable life. Together they had everything they could ever need. His wife mentioned going to church from time to time, but Dan never had much interest in going back. He couldn't see himself as the church-going type. The birth of their first child changed his mind. He figured his daughter needed to be exposed to stories about God, but that was as far as he planned on taking it.

But when the pastor and other men in the church took time to get to know Dan, he began to see a greater need than making sure his little girl learned the words to "Jesus Loves Me." He realized his need for Christ. When asked, Dan can't pick out a sermon or Sunday school lesson that suddenly made all the pieces come together. In fact, the quality of the worship services and other programs of the church played a relatively minor role in his conversion. The biggest factors, which kept him coming back and softened his heart to the gospel, were the relationships he was welcomed into by the church community. No one cared about what he did in the past. They weren't shocked by the handful of details that spilled out. Instead, Dan found himself in the midst of a group of people who genuinely cared about him.

Dan came face-to-face with the best evidence for Christ we can give the postmodern world. Oz will never be changed through programs or evangelism strategies designed to convert strangers. Reaching people in the new millennium demands building authentic relationships through our lives and through our churches. It is not easy. Trying to love people into the family of God means we take the very real risk of being rejected and hurt, but we can't love people and keep them at arm's length. Nor can we love them without getting our hands dirty and leaving ourselves tired and emotionally drained. The love that changes lives gives without expecting anything in return. Yet by doing this, we imitate the evangelism strategy of Jesus, Himself, who loved the world and gave Himself up for her.

CHAPTER FOURTEEN

Coming Out from Behind the Curtain

I don't know why any Christian should have anything to do with movies." As she spoke Elizabeth contorted her face as if she'd just bitten into something sour, but she had already finished her lunch. Her empty tray sat in front of her as she continued, "Some churches don't agree with me, I know, but we shouldn't let the garbage in movies seep into our minds if we're serious about following Jesus. And the same goes for television. There's nothing worth watching." Elizabeth's voice didn't rise with emotion trying to make a point. She spoke in a very matter-of-fact tone as though everyone around her already agreed with her. "We don't watch movies in my home, and my kids only listen to good, Christian music. I can't understand why any serious believer would do anything else."

The pre-lunch teaching session in the youth leadership camp where Elizabeth had volunteered to be a small group leader prompted her comments. This session focused on learning to discern the underlying messages in popular cultures. Several clips from movies and one or two popular television sitcoms played on the video projector screen, after which the session leader asked students to tell him what each said about God and human nature, morality, and salvation.

"That one clip just gave me the creeps," Elizabeth went on. "What was that movie?" she asked her husband. After he told her she continued, "That's right, *Signs*. That sent cold chills down my spine. How could that man say those things about God? I don't understand why that session was part of a discipleship camp. I don't think it belonged here."

Elizabeth isn't alone. She speaks for many believers, and she expresses the age-old tension that we Christians feel as we look at the culture around us. We don't want to swallow everything it dishes out. The worldview of most expressions of popular culture stands in direct opposition to a biblical worldview, along with its ideas of right and wrong. Romans 12:1-2 makes it very clear that followers of Christ are not supposed to think like everyone else. Our minds must be renewed by the transforming power of the Spirit and the Word of God.

At the same time, part of the mandate placed on believers is not only to share salvation with individuals, but to transform the culture as well. Charles Colson calls this the cultural commission, which he places alongside the Great Commission to make disciples. "Salvation does not consist simply of freedom from sin; salvation also means being

> We cannot hide from our culture and change it at the same time.

restored to the task we were given in the beginning—the job of creating culture," he writes. Our task, Colson continues, is not just to save souls but also to "bring all things under the lordship of Christ, in the home and the school, in the workshop and the corporate boardroom, on the movie screen and the concert stage, in the city council and the legislative chamber."[1]

This is the rest of our task as missionaries to Oz, and it is also our dilemma. How can we reshape our culture while remaining unstained by the world? The wizard of Oz couldn't do a thing in the real world as long as he hid behind his curtain. God calls you and me to come out from behind the safety and security of our homes and churches and to begin interacting with our culture in a redemptive way. Jesus told us to be *in* the world but not *of* the world. We cannot hide from our culture and change it at the same time. Nor does the cultural commission allow us to construct our own alternative subculture made just for other believers. Our Lord calls us to extend His lordship over every aspect of our lives. As we do, we not only change our culture, we also reveal the God who is there to the people of Oz.

MEANINGFUL DIALOGUE

Pastor Matt Whickam decided to take a risk. The war against terrorism brought to the forefront the ongoing tension between Christianity and Islam and between Islam and Judaism. This tension didn't play out on the world stage alone. More and more of the members of his church work alongside people of different faiths. "I wanted to find some way to help our people understand the differences between world religions, but I wanted to do it in a way that would open doors for sharing the gospel."

Matt did something that raised more than a few eyebrows and made some members of his congregation question his sanity. On back-to-back Sundays, Matt invited a rabbi and then a leader of the local Islamic community to speak to his evangelical church. However, Matt didn't want to give the impression that the differences between Christianity and other religions didn't exist or that they didn't matter. "I wanted to highlight the differences without debating," Matt said, "and I also wanted our guests to experience genuine Christian love for perhaps the first time."

As members filled the auditorium those two Sundays, they noticed the music stand that served as the church's pulpit was missing. Two chairs took its place. After the worship band left the stage, Matt walked out with the guest speaker. The two sat in the chairs, and for the next forty minutes they engaged in a dialogue. Matt asked questions, which allowed his guest to fully explain exactly what his religion believes and teaches regarding God, the Bible, Jesus, sin, and salvation. On both Sundays, he didn't interrupt his quest's answers nor did he tell them how their ideas didn't match the Bible.

It was a risky move, but by taking it, Matt gave an example to his church of how they need to interact with the culture around them. "It's a fine line we have to walk," Matt told me. "On the one hand we can't swallow hook, line, and sinker what our culture says, but at the same time we can't be belligerent, not if we want to be heard. What I hoped to show our church was how to engage in a meaningful dialogue that will open the door for the gospel."

We need to engage in the same dialogues, not only with people of different faiths, but also with the culture at large. The movies, music, and television shows express many of the beliefs and hopes and fears of the people around us. Our ears need to learn to listen for what they tell us. If we will listen closely, we will hear questions like "Who is God?" in Steven King's book *The Girl Who Loved Tom Gordon* and "What was it like to be the man who put Jesus to death?" in *The Green Mile*. Michael Crichton explores questions of ethics and human depravity in *Jurassic Park* and *Prey*. Listen closely, and you will hear rock band Jimmy Eat World express the postmodern world's yearning for something more than the world offers in their song "Bleed American." M. Night Shyamalan explores the question of faith in a God who allows tragedy in *Signs*. These are but a few examples.

Ideas and questions about God and the Bible and sin and salvation permeate expressions of popular culture. Joining in the dialogue can become a point of common ground with unbelievers, which will allow us to share the gospel in a way they can understand. This is exactly what the apostle Paul did when he met with a group of philosophers on Mars Hill (see Acts 17:16–34). Paul started his discussion of the "unknown God" by quoting one of Athens's own poets, rather than quoting Genesis or Isaiah. He then moved to telling them how the unknown God had revealed Himself through His Son, Jesus. (For more on how to use expressions of popular culture as a bridge to share the gospel, see my article from *Discipleship Journal*, "Reel Conversations" in appendix B.)

A word of warning is necessary. We must also be careful that we do not use the prospects of engaging in dialogue with the culture as an excuse to indulge our flesh.

Watching a movie with explicit sexual images in the name of finding some common ground "so I can share Christ with my neighbor" is wrong. We must strive to be holy, while we also try to understand the people around us and speak with them in a meaningful way. It's a fine line each of us must find.

CHANGE FROM THE INSIDE

If we are to fulfill our mission to Oz to reach individuals and impact the culture as a whole, we must move further out from behind the curtain to engage the culture in meaningful dialogue and begin to speak through it. "Ultimately," Charles Colson said, "to be a redemptive force in popular culture, we must encourage Christians to go beyond being critical and start being creative. . . . In popular culture, as in every field, the best way to reach a nonbeliever is not so much by works that preach Christianity explicitly as by works that express a Christian worldview indirectly."[2] C. S. Lewis also challenges believers to speak through the culture when he writes:

> *Our Faith is not very likely to be shaken by a book on Hinduism, but if whenever we read an elementary book on Geology, Botany, Politics, or Astronomy, we found that its implications were Hindu, that would shake us. It is not the books written in direct defense of Materialism that make the modern man a materialist; it is the materialistic assumptions in all the other books. In the same way, it is not a book on Christianity that will really trouble him. But he would be troubled if, whenever he wanted a cheap popular introduction to some science, the best work on the market was always by a Christian.*[3]

Jonathan Lippmann heeded Lewis's challenge when he started his Grammy nominated band, True Vibe. Trained as a classical musician, Jonathan was one of the founding members of the group 98 Degrees, yet he left the group right before it soared to the top of the charts. "I had only been a believer for about a year," Jonathan said, "and I knew I wasn't spiritually mature enough to handle the pressures and temptations that come with that kind of success. I needed to grow up in the faith." Leaving 98 Degrees did not mean leaving behind the music industry.

With True Vibe, Jonathan wanted to create music that would glorify God, but he didn't want to sing for a Christian audience alone. "I wanted our music to glorify God not only with the content of the lyrics but also with the excellence of the music itself. My goal was for anyone who heard a True Vibe song, believer or nonbeliever, to think our music was as good as anything else out there."

After its formation, True Vibe didn't start off singing in churches. Their first public appearance came in front of over 18,000 people in Indianapolis as they sang the national anthem before the tip-off of a NBA Eastern Conference Finals game between the Pacers and Knicks. In the months that followed, the group appeared on *Late Night with David Letterman* and performed the national anthem for several NFL, NBA, and major league baseball teams, including a *Monday Night Football* game between the Colts and Bills. But their biggest break came when a chance meeting in a Nashville agent's office resulted in the group being invited to tour with Destiny's Child.

"I was a little apprehensive about accepting the invitation," Jonathan said. "I wondered how we would be received by the audience because the message of our songs is so clear. And we were also completely unknown. We'd just finished our first CD when the call came, and we didn't even have anything on the radio yet. I also had a few people in the Christian music industry warn me that we might be perceived as selling out our convictions by touring with a secular group. But I am convinced that we have to go beyond the church audience if we are to get the message of Christ out to the world. The Bible is very clear about that."

"The first night we opened for Destiny's Child the other guys in the group and I were pretty nervous," Jonathan continued. "We were standing just offstage, waiting to go on, when the introduction started with the words, 'The guy who started 98 Degrees . . .' Then we heard the crowd start screaming, and we knew we would have a hearing. But we also knew we would have to prove ourselves. We only had time for three or four songs, so we started with 'Jump, Jump, Jump,' which is blatantly about Jesus. Then we sang a song or two that are more secular yet reflect a positive Christian message. And we always concluded our set with the a cappella song, 'I Live for You.'"

After concerts, group members stuck around to sign autographs for fans. "People asked us about the songs as they came through the line which gave us an opportunity for a quick witness," Jonathan said. "They especially asked about 'I Live for You' which focuses on living our lives totally for Christ. And fans coming through the autograph line would also comment on how nice we were as they met us. Those comments reinforced to me how important it was that we live the message as well as sing it."

At times members of the Christian media asked if the group shared the gospel with the audience during their concerts with Destiny's Child and later with Aaron Carter. Jonathan answered by explaining how the promoters only gave them fifteen minutes for their set, which didn't leave time to say anything. "But the truth of the matter is this," Jonathan said, "the people who came to see Destiny's Child didn't come to be preached to. If we had tried, we wouldn't have been allowed on the stage a second time. But if the music speaks for itself, and the lyrics work, and we pray for people's hearts to be soft, then God will work through it."

Living as a missionary to Oz means more than living a good Christian life in view of our unbelieving friends and neighbors. It demands that we extend Christ's lordship over every part of our lives, letting our talents and abilities actively display the power of the living God. We can't hide behind the safety and security of our homes or churches. The world around us is dead and decaying. God has given to us the message of life. If we don't do something, who will?

In the Arena

Teaching any place other than a public high school is not an option for Jeff. It isn't that he didn't have other choices open to him. He could easily teach in a private school in an upper-class neighborhood or at a Christian school, but if he did he would miss his purpose for becoming an art teacher in the first place. Jeff teaches in a public high school because this is the place God wants him to serve. Even so, he has days when the constant barrage of being on the front lines in the mission to Oz wears him down.

"Sometimes I shake my head and wonder why in the world I ever wanted to teach here," Jeff said. "I'll ask God if He is sure this is *the* place that He wants me. And the answer always comes back the same. So I stop complaining and get back to work."

The job Jeff had out of college was in a private school, but it wasn't one of those upscale academies where the students wear matching uniforms. Instead Jeff taught in a licensed residential center for troubled kids in Texas. All of his students were wards of the court. Some were orphans; others had been removed from their homes because of neglect or abuse. Others simply landed there because the courts had no other place to put them. "Teaching there brought together my love for art and my desire to work with kids who need help," Jeff said. After a couple of years, he moved back to the Midwest to work on his master's degree and began teaching in a public high school.

Jeff's broken up his share of fights, and six or seven years ago he had a student shove a needle into his hand. More than once a student became so upset after being disciplined that as he walked out the door he would turn and say something about coming back and straightening things out. "In light of Columbine, I know what he is inferring," Jeff said, "but I always remember God is the One who put me here. He's still in charge."

The language in his school has changed through the years. "Far out" is not the F-word of choice in school hallways anymore. The way students dress also presents a challenge. Jeff teaches ceramics classes where students sit on stools and lean over pottery wheels while working. "These girls come into class wearing a crop top, leaning over the wheel while their thong underwear hangs out on the back side, and they are putting on a show for all the guys in the class," Jeff sighed. "As a man and a father, you wonder why these girls would want to dress so provocatively, and you wonder why parents would let them out the door dressed like that."

The clothes and the language and the fights and everything else are simply the reality of teaching in a high school. That's part of the culture in which a Christian teacher has to operate. Jeff doesn't just sit by and say nothing, but he also doesn't preach sermons in class about the evils of cursing. "At the beginning of every school year, I tell students about the class and its structure. I tell them straight up that I am a Christian. I make it clear that they can disagree with me, but I don't want to be offended by their language or their stories. I'm open and honest with them, and I expect the same from them. I find when I am honest with my students, they usually return the favor."

Being open and honest with his students is a key part of Jeff's mission in the classroom. He works to see every student as someone who was created in God's image, regardless of how the student acts in class. "I don't know why," Jeff said, "but many times I have a good rapport with students that other teachers can't get along with. I find I can get through to troubled kids that others are tempted to give up on. I think it all comes down to treating students with respect and never looking down on them as somehow inferior. A lot of times I can get through some of the hard, crusty stuff that makes other people regard a student as hopeless. I really value that for it is a key part of me being able to influence the kids I come across."

Everything Jeff said sounded great, but knowing the restrictions placed upon teachers when it comes to openly sharing their faith, I wondered how much of God's truth Jeff would actually be able to share. He just laughed. An art class lends itself to constant conversations flying back and forth around the classroom. While working on sculptures or paintings or stained glass, the kids in his room talk about more than the upcoming Phantom Planet concert. They talk about everything, including all the moral and religious issues of the day. And when they do, Jeff joins in the conversations whether the subject is abortion or capital punishment or drugs or alcohol or God.

Sometimes the conversations take an unexpected turn. One day a few years ago, one of his female students with a reputation for promiscuity came into class and started talking about what she did over the weekend. Suddenly she opened her purse and dumped out a pile of condoms in all sorts of colors and varieties. "I simply told her to put those things away and never bring them back to my class again," Jeff said. "It was a touchy situation, but this also allowed me to talk with her about the choices she was making and the long-term effects those choices would have on the rest of her life. I didn't do this in front of the rest of the class, but waited for a moment when things had quieted down."

Another female student started talking one day about moving in with her thirty-three-year-old boyfriend. Her parents, she said, were fine with the decision. After all, she believed he loved her and would take care of her. "We talked," Jeff said, "and I asked her if she really knew what she was doing. I told her how the only thing she as a seventeen-year-old girl had in common with a thirty-three-year-old man was sex. We talked for a while, and I tried to get her to think about what she was about to do with her life. She didn't believe me and ended up dropping out of school to cook and clean for her boyfriend. But the end result didn't change the fact that I knew God had me there to try to provide some wisdom and godly counsel for her. Whether or not she listened was up to her."

There are times Jeff is able to share God's truth more overtly. Every year he teaches an art history class. "Art history is church history," Jeff told me. The church commissioned paintings and sculptures in a time when most people couldn't read or write. The works of art were a way of communicating the stories of the Bible. Biblical themes play a prominent role in art even today. And when they do, Jeff tells his students the stories from the Bible that inspired the artist's work. He said of the depictions of the Crucifixion, "Some of the pictures are very sanitized, but some are very realistic such as Grunewald's *Crucifixion* which uses green tones and shows Jesus with His skin hanging off to illustrate the gruesomeness of the Cross. I show slides of these different accounts in paintings and compare them with the biblical story. I do the same thing with paintings of Mary and Jesus. I compare the way these themes are depicted through church history and then give the narratives from the Bible."

The method works and is acceptable because he isn't teaching religion. He is teaching history. And since biblical themes played such a prominent role in art through the centuries, they can play a prominent role in his class.

Even though he has the opportunity to actively share God's truth, Jeff knows that one of the most important things he can do for his class is show them a life of integrity. Many of his students don't have any sort of positive, male role model in their lives. They come from homes where fathers are absent, and some come from homes where the man of the house supplies them with drugs and alcohol. What they see in Jeff's life is as important as the words they hear from his mouth.

"A lot of them just tune you out," Jeff said, "but whether they agree or disagree, at least they know where I stand. I don't ever want to be in the place where someone would look at me and say, 'Why didn't you tell me?'" The work doesn't end when a student graduates. Even after they leave school, Jeff sees them and talks with them about their choices and who they are. "I haven't had the privilege of doing it yet, but some of the

Christian teachers I work with have led kids to Christ through these conversations."

Jeff has a life outside of the classroom. He and his wife and their four children witness to neighbors and are very involved in their local church. Jeff has taught Sunday school classes and worked on the church building and done just about anything that needed to be done. Several weekends a year he goes into prisons with the Bill Glass Prison Ministry Team. He's also chaired the trustee board for the local crisis pregnancy center and worked with the teenagers in his church on Sunday nights.

"I have an uncle," Jeff told me, "who will tell me that he thinks I may have missed my calling. He tells me he thinks I should become a full-time Christian minister." Jeff smiled and said, "I already am."

This is what it means to be a missionary to Oz.

Recommended Books

BOOKS OUTLINING THE
HISTORICAL PATH TO POSTMODERNITY

The Abolition of Man, by C. S. Lewis. Written nearly sixty years ago, Lewis's classic foresaw the trends that would usher in the postmodern world. This 121-page book is not an easy read, but it is well worth the effort. This work set me on a course that became *Mission to Oz.*

The God Who Is There, and *Escape from Reason,* by Francis Schaeffer. While you're at it, you might as well read the third book of the trilogy, *He Is There and He Is Not Silent.* Schaeffer broke ground among evangelicals by showing how Christ's lordship extends over the arts and all of culture. Though written in the late sixties and early seventies, the books trace a line that ultimately would eventually lead to postmodernism.

Modern Times: The World from the Twenties to the Nineties, by Paul Johnson. Postmodernism didn't arise in a vacuum. In some ways it is the logical conclusion of the modern age. Johnson's history of the twentieth century reveals what brought us to this point. The book also gives perspective by showing how many of the characteristics of the postmodern world were major factors in the modern world as well. Also check out Johnson's *The Birth of the Modern World Society 1815-1830.* Whenever someone begins talking about how corrupt the world is today, I refer him to this book. Morality at the beginning of the twenty-first century is not very different than it was two hundred years ago.

BOOKS ON POSTMODERNISM

Postmodernism for Beginners, by Jim Powell. This is not a Christian book nor was it written from the perspective of a biblical worldview. Some of the language in it is offensive. However, Powell gives a concise and accurate description of the postmodern world, including a summary of writings and names of people that have shaped this period.

A Primer on Postmodernism, by Stanley Grenz. One of the best Christian books on postmodernism. Gives a very good overview of the thoughts and trends that make up this period of time.

Soul Tsunami: Sink or Swim in New Millennium Culture, by Leonard Sweet. Sweet not only surveys the postmodern landscape, he suggests that these can be great times for the gospel. Like its title, the book at times swirls around and threatens to drown the reader, but it is worth the effort.

If you want to dig even deeper into the thought forms which make up postmodernism, you may want to read the works of Jean Baudrillard, Michael Foucault, and James Derrida. All three are French writers who shaped much of our understanding of the postmodern period. If you tackle their books, remember they write from a purely secular worldview, and their work is not very reader friendly.

A CHRISTIAN RESPONSE TO POSTMODERNISM

As Individuals:

Postmodern Pilgrims and *The Dawn Mistaken for the Dusk,* by Leonard Sweet. The latter is an e-book. Both are short, readable, and practical. If you never read anything else by Sweet, you should read these two books.

Making Sense of the Church: Eavesdropping on Emerging Conversations About God, Community, and Culture, by Spenser Burke, Colleen Pepper, and Stanley Grenz. Burke is the creator of the postmodern ministry Web site www.theooze.com. This book is a snapshot of The Ooze community conversation as it tries to make sense of God in the emerging worldview. It represents a gathering of individuals with different points of view, theologies, life contexts, and feelings.

Beyond Foundationalism: Shaping Theology in a Postmodern Context, by Stanley Grenz. How do we speak the eternal truths of God to a culture that no longer believes in truth? Grenz directs a way. Chapter three alone is worth the price of the book.

As CHURCHES:

Future Church, by Jim Wilson. Jim traveled across the country visiting churches on the cutting edge of ministry to the postmodern world. The book gives great insights into the type of ministry needed for this age and snapshots of how to do it.

The Emerging Church, by Dan Kimball. A detailed example of what a purpose-driven church can look like in a postmodern world.

An Unstoppable Force: Daring to Become the Church God Had in Mind, by Erwin McManus. Leonard Sweet called this the one book he would require every religious leader to read. McManus is pastor of the cutting-edge Mosaic Church in Los Angeles.

Learning to Hear the Message

Ask yourself the following questions as you consider how a movie, television show, or song relates to biblical truth. Considering these questions will prepare you to engage in substantive conversation the next time you ask a friend, "So what did you think about . . ."

THE ROLE OF GOD

God is often characterized in films, though the films rarely portray Him correctly. Hollywood's God ranges from an impersonal force (*Star Wars*) to a semi-powerless deity (many action thrillers that feature the forces of good and evil) to a silent but benevolent Supreme Being that exists to ensure people's happiness (*What Dreams May Come*).

- What kind of God does the film portray? Is He personal, or an impersonal force?

- How does the on-screen God compare with the God of the Bible?
What does the film say about the nature of God? Is He powerful or limited? Good, evil, or morally neutral?
- If the God on-screen were God, indeed, what kind of world would result?

BIBLICAL THEMES

Watch for biblical ideas such as the power of forgiveness, the nature of grace, the corrupting power of sin, and others. *Les Miserables* is a classic example of the power of grace and forgiveness to overcome evil. *Shadowlands* shows how faith in God doesn't guarantee happy endings.

- What spiritual themes did the movie deal with? How does the depiction in the film compare with God's truth?
- Who or what is the source of the spiritual virtues in the film? Do they come from God, or do they flow naturally from basic human nature? How does this compare with your own experience with flesh and blood human beings?
- What do you think about the virtues and vices depicted in the film (e.g., forgiveness, faith, pride, etc.)? How have they shaped your life?

THE HUMAN CONDITION

Many films explore basic human nature, with all its faults and limitations. Such movies touch on everything from our need for other people to survive (*Cast Away*) to the downfall of our pride (*Jurassic Park*) to the longing for an opportunity to undo the mistakes we make in life (*The Sixth Sense*).

- What does the film say about the basic nature of mankind? Are we basically good, or evil? Perfectible, or irreparably flawed?
- What character flaws does the film exploit? Why are people weak in these areas? Why can't we overcome them?
- What does the film say about life on planet Earth? Does life have meaning and purpose, or is it a pointless exercise that ends in death?

THE CONDITION OF THE WORLD

Both *The Matrix* and *The Truman Show* explore the possibility that everything around us is nothing but an illusion, that we people are little more than slaves in this world, though we don't realize it. Their ideas point toward the true nature of reality and mankind's slavery to sin.

- What does the film say about the universe that surrounds us?
- What worldview does the film presuppose? How does that compare with your own? How does it compare with a biblical worldview?
- What in the film made you uncomfortable? Why?
- Would you want to live in the world the film portrayed? Why or why not?

MESSIANIC CHARACTERS

Some films portray a sacrificial hero who lays down his life for someone else. Few movies remind viewers of Jesus' sacrifice more poignantly than *The Green Mile*.

- What role does the central character play in saving or redeeming others in the film?
- Saving others always comes at a great price to the potential savior. What motivated the character to pay such a price? What did he/she stand to gain, if anything? And if the salvation of others cost the character everything with little personal gain, why was the sacrifice made?
- How does the picture of redemption in the film compare with the story of the Cross?

Adapted from the article "Reel Evangelism" published in *Discipleship Journal*, 22, no. 4 (July–August 2002): 27–31.

Notes

Chapter 1: I Have a Feeling We're Not in Kansas Anymore

1. George Barna, *The Second Coming of the Church* (Nashville: Word, 1998), 2.

Chapter 2: Riding the Cyclone

1. William Butler Yeats poem (1922) "The Second Coming."

Chapter 3: One of Everything, Please

1. Allan Bloom, *The Closing of the American Mind* (Simon and Schuster: New York, 1987), 26.
2. http://www.actupny.org/YELL/zine/q_a_s.html.

Chapter 4: Strawberry Fields Lie Just to the Left of the Yellow Brick Road

1. Jim Powell, *Postmodernism for Beginners* (London: Writers and Readers Publishing, 1998), 41.
2. Stanley Grenz, *A Primer on Postmodernism* (Grand Rapids: Eerdmans, 1996), 33.

Chapter 5: Hands-on and High-Touch

1. CBS News, *60 Minutes II,* June 11, 2003.
2. Leonard Sweet, *Postmodern Pilgrims* (Nashville: Broadman and Holman, 2000), 32–33.

Chapter 7: Pay No Attention to That Man Behind the Curtain

1. Francis Schaeffer, *Escape from Reason* vol. 1, *The Complete Works of Francis A. Schaeffer: A Christian World View: A Christian View of Philosophy and Culture* (Wheaton: Crossway Books: 1982), 207.
2. C.S. Lewis, "Answers to Questions on Christianity" *God in the Dock* (Grand Rapids: Eerdmans Publishing: 1970), 58.
3. Francis Schaeffer, *The God Who is There,* vol. 1, from *The Complete Works of Francis A. Schaeffer,* 46.

Chapter 9: The Real World

1. Caleb is a caricature based on conversations with students.
2. Michael Crichton, *Jurassic Park* (New York: Ballantine Paperback edition, 1990), 159.
3. Martin Rees quoted in Marcus Chown, "Anything Goes," *New Scientist* 158, no. 2137 (6 June 1998), 29.
4. John Ankerberg and John Weldon, "The Evolution of Life, Probability Considerations and Common Sense," http://www.johnankerberg.org/Articles/science/SC0502W3.htm.
5. See *New Scientist.* For a complete exploration of the idea go to Max Tegmark's website at http://www.hep.upenn.edu/~max/index.html.
6. Joel Achenbach, *National Geographic,* August 2003, http://magma.nationalgeographic.com/ngm/0308/resources_who.html.
7. Stephen King, *The Stand* (New York: Doubleday, 1978), 260.

Chapter 10: A Reason for Being

1. Francis Schaeffer, *True Spirituality* (Wheaton, Ill.: Tyndale, 1971), 5.
2. Yankelovich survey in *Pastor's Weekly Briefing* (10 September 1999) quoted in Leonard Sweet, *The Dawn Mistaken for the Dusk* (Grand Rapids: Zondervan, 2001), 138, Microsoft Reader and Palm Reader e-book.
3. Rick Warren, *The Purpose Driven Life* (Grand Rapids: Zondervan, 2002), 19.

Chapter 11: Do Something

1. Francis Schaeffer, *The God Who Is There*, vol. 1, *The Complete Works of Francis A. Schaeffer*, 130.

Chapter 12: More than Words

1. George Barna, *The Second Coming of the Church*, (Nashville: Word, 1998), 124.

2. Leonard Sweet, *Postmodern Pilgrims* (Nashville: Broadman and Holman, 2000), xxii.

3. Charles Colson, in an interview with the author, 29 January 2003.

4. Ibid.

5. Francis Schaeffer, *The God Who Is There*, vol. 1, *The Complete Works of Francis A. Schaeffer*, 45.

Chapter 13: Face-to-Face

1. Leonard Sweet, *Soul Tsunami: Sink or Swim in New Millennium Culture* (Grand Rapids: Zondervan, 1999), 22.

2. Francis Schaeffer, *The God Who Is There*, vol. 1, *The Complete Works of Francis A. Schaeffer*, 131.

3. Stanley Grenz as quoted in Rogier Bos, "Engaging Our Postmodern Culture," *Next Wave*, May 1999.

Chapter 14: Coming Out from Behind the Curtain

1. Charles Colson, *How Now Shall We Live?* (Wheaton, Ill.: Tyndale, 1999), 296–97.

2. Ibid., 474.

3. C. S. Lewis, "Christian Apologetics," *God in the Dock*, 93.

SINCE 1894, Moody Publishers has been dedicated to equip and motivate people to advance the cause of Christ by publishing evangelical Christian literature and other media for all ages, around the world. Because we are a ministry of the Moody Bible Institute of Chicago, a portion of the proceeds from the sale of this book go to train the next generation of Christian leaders.

If we may serve you in any way in your spiritual journey toward understanding Christ and the Christian life, please contact us at www.moodypublishers.com.

"All Scripture is God-breathed and is useful for teaching, rebuking, correcting and training in righteousness, so that the man of God may be thoroughly equipped for every good work."
—2 TIMOTHY 3:16, 17

MOODY
PUBLISHERS

THE NAME YOU CAN TRUST®

MISSION TO OZ TEAM

ACQUIRING EDITOR
Mark Tobey

COPY EDITOR
Ali Childers

BACK COVER COPY
Lisa Ann Cockrel

COVER DESIGN
Paetzold Associates

COPY PHOTO
Getty Images

INTERIOR DESIGN
Ragont Design

PRINTING AND BINDING
Bethany Press International

The typeface for the text of this book is
Sabon